First published in the USA in 1977 by
Crescent Books
Distributed by Crown Publishers Inc
One Park Avenue
New York, New York 10016

ISBN 0 517 223686

Published in Great Britain by
Bell & Hyman Limited
37–39 Queen Elizabeth Street
London SE1

First published 1977 by Mills & Boon Ltd,
London.

This reprint © Bell & Hyman Ltd, 1982

Selbie, Robert
    The anatomy of costume.
    1. Costume—History.   I. Title.
      GT511 S44   392 009   77.524

Produced in Spain by
Grijelmo S.A. Bilbao

hgfedcb

The Anatomy of Costume

THE ANATOMY

Contents

4	Introduction	70	French 18th Century
6	Egyptian	74	The Fall of the French Monarchy
10	Biblical	78	Late Georgian, English and American
14	Greek	82	The Directory and the First Empire
18	Roman	86	The Romantic Period 1815–1840
22	Byzantine 400–900	90	The Crinoline
26	Romanesque	94	The American Civil War
30	Early Gothic 1200–1350	98	The Bustle
34	Late Gothic 1350–1450	102	The Pioneer and the Indian
38	Italian Renaissance	106	Fin de Siècle
42	English Tudor	110	Turn of the Century 1900–1914
46	Elizabethan	114	The Great War 1914–1918
50	Spanish Court Dress 16th and 17th Centuries	118	The 1920s
54	Dutch 17th Century	122	The 1930s
58	King Charles I	126	The War Years 1939–1945
62	The Commonwealth 1649–1660	130	The Post-War Era 1945–1960
66	The Restoration	134	The Sixties and After

OF COSTUME

Robert Selbie

Illustrated by Victor Ambrus

CRESCENT BOOKS NEW YORK

Egyptian

French c 1640

French c 1790

Introduction

Clothes today are designed so much for comfort and convenience that we find it difficult to understand people from other centuries, who seem to have dressed deliberately for show, or to attain a fashionable outline, rather than for ease and simplicity of movement. To some extent this impression is a misconception, for our knowledge of what people wore in the past has been gained from statues, frescoes, paintings and very formal photographs. Those who deserved to have their appearance recorded for posterity, or who could afford to do so to gratify their own vanity, were very nearly always dressed up in their best and most lavish attire, so that people in future years could appreciate just how worthy they were.

At the other end of the scale from the expensively dressed aristocracy of the grand portraits were the poorest people, whose clothes were often ragged and filthy versions of what the prosperous had worn fifty or sixty years before. Not surprisingly, there is little pictorial evidence of this. Between the two extremes, in every country, came the ordinary people. They could afford to follow fashions, if not set them, and their taste started trends for their sons and daughters.

It is the "anatomy" of ordinary clothes—their fabric, design and decoration—which gives us a vivid picture of the costume of any age, and there are many sources of information for such details. We can find out what materials were used in Victorian and Edwardian times from Mrs Beeton's wonderful book on household management, in which she writes of "summer dresses of barège, muslin, mohair and other light materials". We know what Lord Byron spent on clothes, and what he sent to the laundry, from the meticulous accounts kept by his steward, Antonio Lega Zambelli, who noted such purchases as "sixty pairs of nankeen or white jean trowsers". We are used to thinking of jean as a modern fabric, whereas its name comes from a type of cloth made in Genoa, or Gènes.

There is a tendency to think of the fashions of the past as "costumes"—something worn by actors to create an impression, unaccountably spotless or artificially dirtied; or something discovered in grandmother's attic trunk, to dress up in on a rainy day, or to wear to a fancy dress party. But records from the earliest times show us that what looks like fancy dress today was everyday clothing once.

American c 1840

German c 1840

Fashions were changed to suit the architecture in which they were worn, and sometimes the architecture was changed to suit the fashions. The high, pointed headdress which women wore in the fifteenth century grew to such fantastic proportions in France that the doors of the Castle of Blois had to be heightened for the ladies to get through comfortably. When Joan of Arc arrived at the Court she was ridiculed because of her clothes and her little hat.

Exaggerations in fashion, some of which started as the whims of the very rich and then became everyday wear, were often the result of individual shortcomings. For example, Charles VIII of France, who had six toes on one foot, wore specially designed shoes to cover the deformity. This gave rise to the stylish, square-toed shoes of Tudor England.

An important aspect of the anatomy of dress is the use of fabric, and the origins of the different materials. In the Middle and Far East, and in the southern hemisphere, people have always dressed sensibly, taking into account the temperature and the way of life. So we find that the Ancient Egyptians wore transparent, gauzy linens, and the Ancient Greeks wore very little. Silk was known in the Far East long before it came to the West. When such exotic materials were brought home by the soldiers of the Roman Empire they were enthusiastically adopted by those who could afford them. In the Middle East the desert people have always worn voluminous abas and burnouses, often in dark colours or black. However, the adaptation of styles of clothing to suit the climate is a comparatively recent development in the West. Europeans and inhabitants of other northern countries appear to have worn clothes designed for mild weather, and then added or subtracted a layer at a time, depending on the temperature. The introduction and popularity of lightweight, synthetic materials in the West created opportunities for new, different and sometimes shocking styles, especially for warmer weather.

Over the centuries international travel has brought innovations in fashion, introduced new fabrics and styles, and subtly altered costume from one country to another. The costume of today, in any country, has received a myriad of influences and will, in turn, be altered to shape tomorrow's clothing.

Egyptian

Gold necklace and pendant

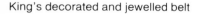

King's decorated and jewelled belt

The popular image of Ancient Egypt is more or less confined to such famous rulers as Queen Hatshepsut, the Pharaoh Tut-ankh-amun and the legendary Queen Cleopatra. It is perhaps difficult to appreciate that these three monarchs ruled during the second half of the span of Ancient Egyptian civilization, after Egypt had been a cultural force for fifteen hundred years.

Throughout their civilization the Ancient Egyptians are known to have been very religious, and their belief in life after death resulted in beautifully decorated tombs and temples. Kings and nobles were put to rest in tombs, surrounded by their wigs, jewels and robes for the afterlife. The discovery of these tombs has enabled us to know more of life in 1500 B C than we do of some periods in more recent history.

Egyptian civilization was based on a very strict class system, with the pharaoh at its head, supported and sometimes dominated by his nobles and priests. The professional classes followed them, then came the labourers and the slaves.

Clothing was very lightweight and was designed for con-venience, as well as indicating the rank and importance of the wearer. The basic garment for men was a simple loincloth, worn by all ranks as an under-garment. Slaves and labourers seldom wore anything else, but the professional and upper classes could also wear a short or medium length linen skirt, either simply draped or with a stiff, almost kite-shaped pleat in front. To this was added an ornamented belt with a wedge-shaped tab, often made of leather with rich embroidery or jewellery. A slave might wear a simpler version of the belt made from cloth, with his master's name marked on it.

This very scanty attire was considered enough for ordinary work, for leisure or for sport. Even the pharaoh would wear no more than a loincloth, prob-ably embroidered with gold, and a short transparent skirt when he went out hunting. The beautiful gilded statuette of King Tut-ankh-amun, now in the Cairo Museum, shows him wearing a short, finely pleated skirt and an elaborate belt with the jewelled tab reaching almost to his knee. He also wears a heavy jewelled collar and the red crown of Upper Egypt.

For more formal occasions men wore tunics of varying lengths, the fineness of the material depending on the rank of the wearer. The poorer classes would wear knee length tunics of coarse linen. The nobles and priests, however, had fine, almost transparent tunics reaching nearly to the ankle. These were either girded with jewelled belts or allowed to remain loose. On state or high religious occa-sions a member of the nobility would wear a voluminous robe in a patterned transparent material over a tight-fitting, long under tunic. Whenever the tunics or robes were belted, the fullness of the material was always drawn to the front. Occasionally the robes were worn entirely unsewn and undraped.

One everyday costume accessory, worn by both men and women, was the collar. It was a wide, flat band which extended from the base of the throat to the shoulders. Rows of coloured beads made of clay, semi-precious stones, gold and glass were strung on wires to make the collars, which were

Worker in loin cloth

Official in skirt over loin cloth c. 1460 BC

King in stiff loin clot[h] crown and broad co[llar]

Man's hairstyle

Woman's hairstyle and vulture headdress, with broad collar

Noblewoman's tight-fitting dress with shoulder straps

worn with the simple skirts as well as with the more complicated patterned robes.

It was fashionable for men to be clean shaven, with few exceptions, such as while travelling or in mourning, or at war—and even then it was unusual to see an unshaven officer.

As the civilization grew more sophisticated, a fashion arose for shaving and polishing the head; and wigs, simple to begin with, but eventually more highly coloured and elaborate, became an important item in the wardrobes of the rich and powerful people surrounding the court. Today it is still possible to see the styles of Egyptian wigs in the elaborately plaited hair of South African Zulu women.

The fabric most suited to the warm, dry climate was linen, which ranged in quality from the very rough material worn by the peasants to the sheer gauze favoured by the aristocracy. Sometimes slaves would wear leather garments, and leather was made into protective clothing for soldiers. Vegetable fibres other than flax were occasionally used. Wool, however, was not seen in any great quantity until

the Roman occupation, and, indeed, the sheep was considered an unclean animal, and the use of its wool for clothing was not encouraged.

Animal skins were sometimes used for cloaks, and the Great Priest wore a leopard skin over his pleated fine linen skirt.

Women's clothes were very similar to men's, and often equally scanty and revealing. The Ancient Egyptians do not seem to have been prudish, and the girl dancers would wear nothing but a belt of gold and jewels, and heavy jewelled earrings. Even a nurse helping a doctor with his work would think nothing of removing her tunic so that she would not soil or tear it.

A fashionable woman liked her complexion to be as pale as possible, and Egyptian women created many recipes for achieving this effect. Queen Nitocris believed in a daily bath and frictions with scented oils to avoid sunburn. Make-up was an important item in any woman's household, though some of the ingredients seem positively harmful. The pale creamy base colour which was used on the

face, for instance, had a lead carbonate content.

The simplest garment for women was an ankle length skirt, with a cord around the waist to draw in the fabric snugly. Over this cord would be worn an ornamental belt with decorated or jewelled ends. This was often considered enough, though some women wore semi-circular capes over their shoulders. With or without the cape, the deep jewelled collar was usually worn.

Women also wore tunics like the men, but they were usually full length, and fairly form-fitting. The ladies had their own version of the robe, cut very full from the fine, gauzy linen and then gathered in front and held with the belt placed very high, giving an effect almost like the nineteenth century *Empire* line.

Both men and women either went barefoot or wore simple sandals, often beautifully decorated. In addition to their wide, jewelled collars the Egyptians wore a good deal of other jewellery—bracelets, anklets, rings and pendants. Earrings seem generally to have been confined to dancing girls.

Girl in long narrow skirt with bead decoration

Priest in ceremonial leopard skin and pleated skirt

Dancing slave girl wearing jewellery and headband

Colours

The predominant colour for clothes in Ancient Egypt was white, in dazzling contrast to the black of hair and wigs. Black does not seem to have been used for clothes, but most other colours were, each with its own religious significance. Red was the only unpopular colour, being thought wicked and violent. Magenta was permissible for robes and, as they became more fantastic, for wigs as well. The pharaoh's Northern crown was more terracotta colour than red. A great many bright colours were used in the embroidery that bordered the robes and skirts. These were enriched by brilliantly coloured semi-precious stones, enamels, pottery beads, and drops of gold and silver.

Cosmetics

The care and decoration of the face and body was a very important part of the daily routine for fashionable women. Daily massage was recommended to keep slim, and pumice stone was used on the elbows and knees to soften the skin. The body could be rubbed with perfumed oils. At one time there was a fashion —for both men and women—of wearing on the head a little cone of perfumed grease, which would melt in the heat and allow the scent to run down over the wig and the body. When a woman had applied a base coat of white make-up, she would colour her lips with orange lipstick, putting a little of the same colour on her cheeks. She would then concentrate on making up her eyes. The upper and lower eyelids would be shaded with green powder, the eyebrows lengthened and coloured with grey antimony, and the eyes outlined and enlarged with black kohl.

Jewellery

Both men and women wore a great deal of jewellery, often made of gold or other precious metals. Cheaper materials were given greater value by the beauty of the jeweller's work. The true precious stones—ruby, diamond, sapphire and emerald—were unknown, but amethyst, turquoise, garnet and lapis lazuli were used in great profusion. Lapis lazuli was the most sought after, as it was not found in Egypt. In addition to the large collar, royalty, or men of high rank, might wear a flat pectoral ornament. It was made of gold and enamel and hung on a gold chain over the collar. Both sexes wore bracelets of gold and enamel, and could also wear anklets of precious metal. A soldier might be awarded a flat golden ornamental jewel in the shape of a fly if he distinguished himself in battle. Signet rings were signs of officialdom, worn on any finger or the thumb. The seal was cut with the wearer's name or official symbol.

Wigs and Hair

A bald, shining head was thought a sign of nobility. The fashionable wore wigs of real hair. Originally these were black, but later on appeared in a variety of unlikely colours. They could be gilded, or ornamented with gold thread, and might be covered with a cloth wig-cover. If the real hair was worn, it would be cut in a round shape following the lines of a man's head. Women sometimes copied men's styles, but usually wore their hair longer, parted in the middle and put into fine plaits with tightly curled ends. Men were clean-shaven, although a beard was a sign of distinction. The gods were thought to have beards, and as the kings considered themselves children of the gods, they wore perfumed false beards on ceremonial occasions. Even Queen Hatshepsut, after she had assumed the rank of pharaoh, wore the false "beard of the gods" for special ceremonies.

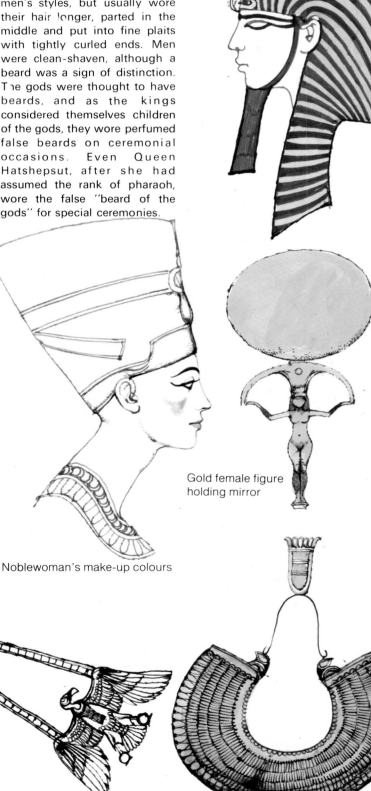

Striped cloth wig cover and ceremonial fake beard

Gold female figure holding mirror

Noblewoman's make-up colours

Musician's grease head-cone designed to melt gradually

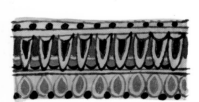

Material with typical colour and pattern

The Vulture of Egypt pendant of kings

Broad gold neck collar

red Crown of Egypt
with cobra head

vulture headdress made
of different coloured stones

broad decorated collar
of stones and beads

broad decorated collar
of stones and beads

king's heavy belt
decorated with stones

tight-fitting transparent
dress with thin
shoulders straps

lightweight skirt
gathered in front

decorative ribbon

light sandals

King and Queen of Egypt

Combined vulture and cobra
pendant

**Be not influenced by fine clothes
And refuse not him that is in rags.**

Amen-em-apt (c 700 BC)

Scarab ring

Biblical

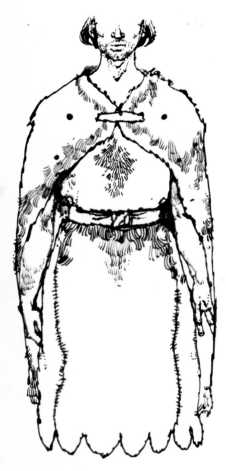

Biblical period fur cape and undergarment

The histories of the nations of Palestine and the Middle East in Biblical times were interwined, producing a mixture of clothing styles. Delilah and Solomon would have copied the fashions of the Assyrians; Samson would have dressed like the Israelites; King Ahab and his wife, Jezebel, would have been influenced by the splendid court of Nineveh; and the three wise men would have travelled to Bethlehem in Persian clothes.

The Mediterranean climate of Palestine required clothes that were designed for warmth, unlike the light Egyptian fashions. There were no rules against the wearing of wool, and the earliest garments, from Chaldean times, were simply sheepskins sewn together and held around the waist with a leather thong. Sometimes a cloak of sheepskin was worn over one shoulder. In early Babylonian times a large, fringed woollen shawl was worn draped around the body and over one shoulder. Women wore a very simple, straight tunic, similar to the Egyptian one. They sometimes wore a short fringed cape as well.

With the rise of Assyria as a power, the cultural influence of Babylon was mixed with Assyria's military influence, culminating in the glittering, cruel court of Nineveh. Although the basic garments worn by the Assyrians remained simple, changing only in small details over centuries, the ornamentation was lavish.

The tunic was still a common item of clothing though the Persian tunic was styled with long sleeves and without a belt, which had been an essential part of Assyrian dress.

The Persians also wore a robe, resembling that worn by the Egyptians, but made in heavier materials—lightweight wool, or even silk. The robe seems to have been the preserve of the king and important nobles, and was worn over a tunic and trousers. It could be drawn up and tucked into a narrow belt to keep it out of the way.

So much less is known about women's clothes of this period because, like the Assyrians before them, the Persian artists used their skills to glorify the male of the species. Their carvings and beautifully coloured, glazed tile panels record military and sporting scenes rather than domestic events. It is probable that the Persian women wore a tunic like their Assyrian predecessors, perhaps with short sleeves, and a narrow shawl.

Both men and women wore some jewellery still, but not nearly as much as had once been the custom. A great deal more restraint was shown in the adornment of costumes with jewels, embroidery, patterns and fringes.

The Israelites, who had been the more or less unwilling recipients of all these splendid and changing fashions, were basically a desert people. Their loose, original dress, with its all-covering garments and its draped headdress to protect the wearer from the sun, wind and sand, can still be seen in present day Morocco and Algeria.

The art of weaving cloth in wide strips of different colours was practised by the Hebrews, and Joseph's "coat of many colours" may have been made from such material.

The men generally wore very simple clothes. A short-sleeved tunic, usually ankle length, often fringed round the hem, was worn with a rectangular shawl.

Shepherd wearing early skin garment tied with belt

Sumerian official in Babylonian dress wearing turban-like headdress

Babylonian woman with material draped around body

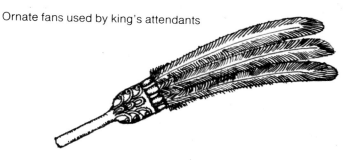
Ornate fans used by king's attendants

Assyrian king's cylindrical headdress

Man's tasselled shawl with decorated belt

The plain tunic, in wool or linen, or even in supple leather, with short sleeves, was worn by every man. Its length varied depending on the activity of the wearer. A nobleman out hunting, needing freedom of movement, would wear a tunic with the hem cut up in a V shape, probably trimmed with rich, gold fringe. It is believed that a person's rank could be judged by the length of the fringe on his clothes.

Longer tunics were worn for less strenuous pastimes, combined with a less full version of the earlier shawl, one end of which was tucked into the belt and the other carried around the body and draped over the shoulder.

A feature which is seen repeatedly on sculptures and panels of the period is the double belt. A wide band of leather went first around the waist and was held in place by a much narrower leather strip on top, which might have a richly carved gold clasp. A nobleman would wear a gold, jewelled collar, much narrower then the Egyptian collar, and matched with bracelets at the wrist and sometimes on the upper arm.

Assyrian women wore a tunic very similar to the men's, though the sleeves were three-quarter length. Over this was worn a large, rectangular shawl with a fringe.

The Assyrian influence lasted in Palestine until 606 B C, when Nineveh was destroyed, and for a short time the power was transferred to a new capital, Babylon. There was little change in the taste for luxury in clothes, however, until the Persian king, Darius, took control of the ancient world. The Hebrews, many of whom had been living in Persia during the intolerant Assyrian rule, were permitted back into Palestine, bringing with them Persian styles in clothing.

Trousers were introduced from Persia, and for the first time became a regular feature of men's clothes. They were worn with either a full length or a short coat with which a man would also wear a hood, designed to cover the neck and chin.

Sometimes a man would wear a broad leather belt over his tunic, or, later on, a belt from a rich embroidered material. In time, a fashion grew for wearing two tunics, an under tunic of fine linen, and a top tunic of wool. The woollen tunic had wide sleeves reaching to the elbow.

A long, loose coat called an aba could be worn, and similar garments are still seen in Palestine.

Hebrew women wore a sleeveless, rather loose tunic belted around the hips. Over this went a gown, almost full length, with long, open sleeves, and on top of that a woman could wear a voluminous version of the man's aba. If they valued their reputation, women always kept their heads covered. Their hair was done in elaborate braids and decorated with gold ornaments. On top of the hair was worn a cap made from some rich material, perhaps covered with sequins. Finally the head was wrapped in a large scarf with an embroidered border. Some women preferred a vast scarf of white gauze.

Throughout the Babylonian and Assyrian times, and to a lesser degree the Persian, both men and women put on as much jewellery as they conveniently could, though in strict Hebrew practice jewellery was worn only by women. There is mention in the Bible of bracelets, rings, crowns and necklaces.

Assyrian man wearing cone hat and tasselled shawl over long under-tunic

Assyrian lady with diadem in hair, wearing decorated shawl over long tunic

Persian warrior in long trousers, headdress and armour

Hebrew woman wearing aba over long gown

Headgear

As far back as 2001 B C a small, round cap was being worn, which formed the prototype for many other kinds of caps and turbans later on. It is still the basis for the wrapped turban worn in Palestine today. Assyrians wore a rather deeper version of this cap, and the king's hat always had a point on top. Sometimes a narrow ribbon was tied round the brow. The ends fell down the wearer's back and finished with simple tassels.

Assyrian man's
truncated cone hat

Sumerian girl's hairstyle
and headdress of stones

A Persian man's hair and beard,
clipped with hot tongs

Hair and Beards

Assyrian men wore their hair long and bushy, and usually waved and set to achieve a formal look. It is possible that wigs were worn if the natural hair was not adequate to achieve the fashionable corrugated effect. Most men had long, elaborately curled beards, cut off square. Women's hair was set in complicated plaits and braids. It was often intertwined with gold wire and decorated with other gold ornaments set with jewels or semiprecious stones. The Persian men wore their hair slightly shorter, but still tightly curled, and their beards were often pointed or cut round.

Soldiers

The soldiers in the early Assyrian period wore knee length chainmail tunics, in much the same shape as the everyday garments. Their helmets were made of bronze or brass, and could be inlaid with the ever popular decoration. The helmets were often plain, pointed caps, sometimes surmounted with a short horsehair crest. Daggers would be carried tucked into the belt on the right side of the body, and a sword was hung on a diagonal sword belt.

Jewellery

In addition to their love of decoration on materials, the Assyrians wore an enormous amount of heavy jewellery. Carvings and tiles show both men and women wearing bracelets on their wrists, armlets on their upper arms, anklets, crowns, many rings and elaborate earrings. The Persians showed more restraint. While both sexes continued to wear jewellery, it was used much more sparingly. The designs on their fabrics were much less florid. Some of their motifs were borrowed from the Egyptians, and the figures of the lion and the bull were favourite decorative subjects.

Sumerian queen's necklace
of gold, cornelian, and
lapis lazuli

Materials

The colours used at this time were white, black, green, red and a sort of reddish purple, the purple of Tyre. The Middle Eastern nations did not seem to have the same superstition about red as did the Egyptians, and contemporary tiles show it to have been a popular colour. The Assyrians decorated all their fabrics with so many patterns and motifs that it was unusual to find a plain material. The patterns might be woven into a woollen fabric, or embroidered on it in gold thread, painted on leather or inlaid into metal surfaces such as armour. Fringe was used everywhere—on shawls, tunics and on the ends of hat ribbons. Sometimes tassels were put on the corners of the shawls.

Accessories

Persian men, who were very elegant, would carry long walking sticks with them. They might even carry flowers in their hands. A slave could carry an umbrella over his mistress or master. These umbrellas were also attached to the backs of chariots, or held by slaves standing behind the drivers. Large leather and feather fans and flywhisks made from horsehair, with ivory or gold handles, were also carried by the slaves to protect their owners from heat and insects.

Fans used in court

Persian warrior in pointed
helmet and plated armour

bow

decorated quiver
for arrows

turban-like coronet

lance

gold bracelets

belt placed below the ribs

long, loose tunic with
full-length sleeves

stockings

leather shoes

The royal bodyguard of Persian archers

gold earring

gold necklace

gold bracelets

long tunic

fringed shawl

Strong shoes with upturned toes

**She doted upon the Assyrians her neighbours,
captains and rulers clothed most gorgeously...**

Ezekiel 23:12

Gold and lapis lazuli headdress of
leaves and flowers, and large
gold earrings

Greek

Girded peplos

It has been said that the last six centuries B C share with the nineteenth and twentieth centuries the distinction of being the only periods in the history of costume in which the women's fashions were more important than the men's.

In Ancient Greece the men wore as little as possible and, therefore, it is better to consider women's clothing first, as being the more complicated.

The guiding principle of the Greek way of life was an appreciation of truth. As a direct result of this the Greeks expressed themselves with great simplicity in art and in fashion. Basically, both men and women were restricted to two garments, the chiton and the himation. In fact, these were nothing more than rectangular pieces of material. However, the way in which they were gathered and draped required great care, taste, and, as the material was often used lavishly, a good deal of management to avoid getting tangled up in the folds.

In very early times the basic dress for women was the peplos, a piece of material wrapped around the body and pinned at the shoulders with large spikes of gold or other precious metal. Because these pins became dangerous objects in the hands of infuriated women, laws were brought against their use. It would have been a pin of this kind which Oedipus took from his dead mother's garments to put out his own eyes.

The peplos developed into the chiton: two rectangular pieces of material, either linen or cotton, which were held together along one of the long sides with clasps, brooches, or, at a later date, buttons, thereby causing the material to fall straight down in front. The fabric was longer than the height of the wearer so that all the fullness could be drawn up and held by the girdle to form the kolpos, a sort of bulge of material around the waist.

There were three ways of girdling this form of chiton, which was known as the Ionic chiton. The most straight forward was a band of ribbon encircling the waist; but it was also possible to take a longer ribbon round the waist and then pass it over the shoulders, round the back again and tie it in front; or to cross it over the chest and circle the waist before tying a bow in front. Whichever way was used, the spare material was pulled up through the ribbon to form the kolpos. Sometimes, if it was necessary to shorten the chiton even further to make walking or running easier, the girdle was continued around the hips, and the extra length of the skirt was tucked into it.

The Doric chiton, worn over the same period of time as the Ionic, was much more like the old fashioned peplos, but without the murderous pins. The Doric chiton was one piece of material, thirty-eight centimetres longer than the wearer's height taken from the shoulder. The top part was folded over and it was then put around the body. The top edges were held together with brooches at the shoulders, and the back of the garment was brought over the shoulders to join the front. It was held at the waist by a simple ribbon belt; although the ladies of Sparta sometimes wore the chiton unbelted, which caused a good deal of scathing comment, for the garment was usually left open down one side.

A garment usually worn with

Girl wearing chiton, with himation round her shoulders

The Ionic chiton

Girl wearing a of chiton

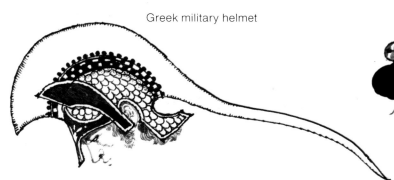

the Ionic chiton was the himation, an oblong piece of linen or woollen material nearly five metres long and banded with one of the formal patterns which the Greeks loved. There were many different ways of wearing the himation: as a cloak on its own, or a combined cloak and head-covering, or with one end over the shoulder and the other draped over the opposite arm. A great deal of time and attention was spent by fashionable women arranging the folds of the himation attractively, and they would stand in formal attitudes designed to show the drapery.

Ordinary people wore dull colours, greens, greys and browns, but a great range of other colours was known: the rich Tyrian purple, "the dye of dyes", made from a kind of shellfish, red, yellow, saffron, emerald and apple green. It is thought that the Greeks had no knowledge of a blue dye, though the colour blue had been known since before 1400 B.C. Pure white was favoured by the aristocracy.

The basic costume for the Greek man was nothing at all.

Athletes and gymnasts would exercise naked, and even soldiers went into battle wearing no more than the chlamys, a short cloak which was worn enveloping the left arm and side, held by a brooch on the right shoulder.

Men's clothes were very similar to woman's, and the simplest garment was a short chiton. Made of a perfectly plain piece of material with fringed edges, the chiton was worn under one arm with the other side pinned on the opposite shoulder. It was left open down the side and belted around the waist with a ribbon. It is thought that the fringe seen in representations of this chiton is nothing more than the unhemmed edge of the material. The short chiton came to just above the knee. Later on it developed into a slightly more elaborate version, with the top edge held to form sleeves, and with simple decoration around the edges.

A variation of the plain fabric worn by both men and women was a "crinkled" chiton. Fine linen could be treated in such a way as to form tiny zig-zag pleats, which were confined to the top of the chiton while the

fullness of the skirt fell into folds.

Older men could wear a longer chiton, which reached to the ankles. This was also worn by charioteers, for whom the length was useful as protection for their legs. A charioteer would wear his chiton belted close to his body so that the folds would not impede his actions.

The himation was also worn by men, either over a chiton or, in the case of philosophers, stoics and sages, on its own. This symbolized the simplicity of their lives. The garment was worn with one end draped over the left arm; the material was then passed behind the body, across the front, and the other end draped over the same arm.

A man's character and breeding could be judged by the way in which he draped his himation, and the arrangement of the material was the subject of endless care. A good deal of practice and concentration was necessary to keep the garment properly draped, for no pins or fasteners were used. Wearing the himation became a studied art, as it was the custom to throw it off and put it on again quickly

Charioteer in long chiton

Man wearing chiton and himation with broad sun-hat

Left: soldier in short himation. Right: philosopher in elaborately draped himation

Jewellery

In the early years of the Greek civilization the use of jewellery maintained the simplicity which controlled other aspects of daily life. It was unusual to see a man wearing any jewel other than a gold signet ring, perhaps set with an engraved stone of cornelian, quartz, or jasper. A woman would wear finely worked gold brooches, which were rarely set with stones, but valued for the beauty of the craftsmanship. Later on, as with many civilizations before and since, increased prosperity brought an increase in outward show, and both men and women covered themselves in gold and jewels. The Archon of Athens, Solon, who lived from about 638 B C to about 558 B C brought in a number of laws designed to curb the extravagance in dress and ornament, but seemingly without success. Women might wear necklaces, earrings designed to produce a tinkling sound as the wearer walked, bracelets, rings, and pins in their clothes or their hair. There was a fashion among young men to wear a single earring, and even some children wore a ring in the right ear.

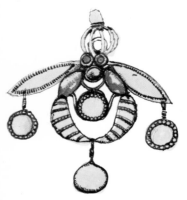

Above: Cretan pendant
c. 17th century BC

Hair and Headgear

For the first 150 years or so of the Greek Age men wore their hair long, dressed in elaborate ways. It was usually encircled by a ribbon or band, and allowed to fall in plaits or ringlets. It was the custom in time of war to cut off these long plaits and offer them to the gods. The Persian Wars brought in a fashion for short hair, which lasted for about a hundred and thirty years. Later, reaction against encroaching Roman influence made men grow their hair long again, though not as long as in the early years. Hats were considered degenerate, except for the petasos, a round cap with a wide brim which could be turned up to form various shapes.

The Stephane

A headdress commonly seen on women in the sixth and fifth centuries B C was a band of gold or bronze rising to a point in the front, which was known as the stephane. Later on it was worn further to the back of the head and stood rather away from it, like a tiara. It could be in plain gold, or have engravings or enamel work on it.

Above right: long hairstyle
from early days of Greek Age
Right: short hairstyle after
the Persian Wars

Lady's small hat, the tholia

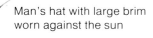

Man's hat with large brim
worn against the sun

Warrior's bronze leg-guard

Patterns and Motifs

The earliest known patterned material dates from the fifth century B C, and shows figures of ducks. The Greeks used all-over patterned fabrics, and many motifs to edge their garments—rosettes, key pattern, acanthus, dentil, egg-and-dart and laurel.

Boots and Shoes

It was still quite customary for people to go barefoot, though a large variety of boots and shoes and sandals were made and worn. Sandals could be made of leather, with cork soles that could be given greater thickness if the wearer thought he needed extra height. High boots were worn by horsemen, and were laced up the front to just below the knee. Feet and shoes were of great importance, and nicknames were given to people who started fashions. Oedipus was so called because his name meant "swollen foot".

Different types of sandals

gold earrings

stephane

himation

crinkled chiton

girdle

himation

knee-length chiton

sandals

Cretan jewellery

Why, they're the very things I hope will save us,
Your saffron dresses and your finical shoes,
Your paints, and perfumes, and your robes of gauze.

Aristophanes: Lysistrata (trans. B. B. Rogers) (c 411 BC)

Decoration from a Greek dress

Roman

The history of Roman costume divides neatly into two periods: the Republican era of 753 B C to 29 B C, and the Imperial years from 29 B C to A D 400. The differences in dress fall into almost the same time spans. Dignified simplicity characterized the days of the Republic, and appalling vulgarity reflected the decadent Empire.

Many of the most usual garments were similar to those worn in Greece during the same period. The outstanding exception was the toga, a garment originally worn by both men and women. It was the most easily recognizable item in the wardrobe of an Ancient Roman. During the first two centuries of Rome's existence the toga appears to have been practically the only garment worn by both sexes, irrespective of rank. Its only distinguishing factor was the material from which it was made. The highest class wore togas of the finest wool in its natural colour. The lowest wore either coarse cloth or a kind of thin felt.

As time went by, the garment went out of fashion for women. Its use was denied to peasants when it began to take on a symbolic significance for men.

There seem to have been about eight different styles of togas, each with its own meaning, by the time the fashion became a purely male preserve. The most simple was the toga pura, which denoted the freedom of the Roman citizen. A version of the same style was the toga virilis, which youths between fourteen and sixteen would adopt on the feast of the Liberalia, on 17 March. Young nobles had their own version of this, the toga praetexta, which had a narrow band of purple or scarlet around the edge.

There was the toga ornamentum; the bleached white toga candida, which was worn by candidates for public office; the toga trabea, worn by a priestly sect—it was striped white and scarlet, and had a purple band all around; the toga pulla, which was black and worn for mourning; and the toga picta, which was an official garment, usually richly embroidered—it was worn by generals making triumphal entries, or by provincial governors when in office. Pontius Pilate, for example, would have worn the toga picta.

The toga was simply a crescent-shaped piece of material with one straight edge, some four and a half to five and a half metres long and one to two metres at its widest point. Although it was sometimes worn on its own, an undergarment called a subligaculum, a simple loincloth, could be worn as well. This was later replaced by a tunic, short at first but gradually becoming longer.

Called the colobium, or tunica, it could be worn either by itself or with a toga. Sometimes two or three tunics were worn. The Emperor Octavius, who was particularly sensitive to cold, was known to wear four at the same time. The tunica in its earliest form was always white, and known as the tunica alba. Later on, different colours were used, usually pale yellow, fawn or shades of brown.

In the first century A D members of the Equestrian Order wore purple stripes down the sides of their tunicas. The stripes were known as the Angustus Clavus, and were a badge of rank. But, like many other things, the style lost its significance when non-military people took

Back view of toga with edge decoration

Older type toga with red edging

Man making a sacrifice, wearing the Toga Praetexta

Philosopher wearing warm cloak, pallium

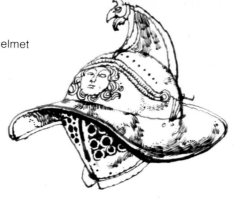
Gladiator's bronze helmet

Cloack decorated with
brightly coloured bands

it up as a fashion. Stripes appeared as a decoration on everyday clothes, sometimes taking the form of a band of beautiful embroidery rather than a stripe of solid colour. In the fifth century this band of embroidery was shortened on men's tunics so that it just spanned the shoulders. This form of the Clavus is the origin of the shoulder straps and epaulettes of modern military and civilian uniforms.

Julius Caesar was assassinated in 44 B.C. and the Emperor Octavius was given the title of Augustus in 29 B.C. A number of emperors followed, including Nero, Hadrian and Trajan. Between AD 96 and 180 Rome's prosperity reached a peak from which it slowly descended. The decline was accompanied by an increase in luxury, decadence, cruelty and crime.

The toga, which became more and more elaborate, with gold embroidery in the shape of circles, stars or suns, gradually went out of favour. As the pace of daily life increased. the folds of the material were found to be inconvenient. Finally, the toga became the official robe of the emperor and was worn over

a long tunic, which was also lavishly decorated.

Fashion-conscious Romans introduced styles from foreign countries, regardless of public opinion. One such garment was a calf length tunic called a dalmatica, which had long, loose sleeves. Emperor Commodus, who was known for his eccentric ways, caused a considerable fuss when he appeared in public in a dalmatica. It was nothing to the storm of protest which arose when Heliogabalus, in AD 218, made an official appearance in a full length, flowing gown with wide, oriental sleeves. If the description of this appearance is to be believed, the Emperor's gown was of sumptuous purple silk, heavily embroidered with gold suns. He wore on his head a many layered gold tiara, and was covered with priceless jewels and swathed in ropes of pearls. His face was made up with pink and white paint, with the eyebrows tinted black.

In the days of the Republic women's clothes were of great simplicity and more or less followed their Greek counterpart. They wore a version of the Ionic chiton, now called a stola,

and over that the palla, which was much the same as the Greek himation. The Roman women did, however, wear an undergarment—a simple rectangle sewn up into a tube and pinned on the shoulders like a chiton.

The materials used were similar to those used in Greece, but weaving techniques had improved over the years, and linen and woollen fabrics were very fine indeed. Cotton first made its appearance in Rome in about 180 B.C. Silk was also known about that time, introduced by the armies returning from their conquests in the East. The cost of such rare material was astronomical, and it was, therefore, much sought after.

The terrifying lapses of taste which the men of Rome committed during the years of the Empire were easily matched by the Roman women. The palla was sometimes worn in an exaggerated fashion, long enough to be wound around the body several times, and then put over the shoulders with the ends trailing on the ground. Embroidery, jewellery, silks and costly muslin from India were all used with a lavish vulgarity.

The toga at the end
of the Empire

Girl wearing bikini-type
undergament, strophium

Girl in tunica and cloak

Woman wearing coloured
shawls over tunica

Jewellery

So much jewellery was worn during the days of the Roman Empire that laws had to be passed to limit its use. One such law forbade unmarried women to wear precious stones or pearls, with the result that the marriage rate increased noticeably. Pins and brooches were made in a variety of precious metals, and often set with jewels or formed in the shape of animal's heads. Jewelled ornaments were very popular for fashionable women to wear in their hair. Earrings were worn by both sexes, though the Emperor Alexander Severus was against the habit for men. Bracelets were worn by men and women, sometimes of gold or silver, but often of three or four rows of pearls bound together with gold, or golden coils in the shape of a serpent. Fashions in jewellery were influenced by the spoils that the soldiers brought back from their various foreign conquests, and at one time the heavy gold bracelets and rings from Britain were in great demand. Elegant people wore several of these rings on each finger, and the gold bracelets became so huge that dishonest dealers would fake them out of paste and pass them off as the genuine article.

Armour

A Roman general would wear, first of all, the subligaculum or loincloth, over which he would put a short tunic. His main armour would consist of a brass or bronze breastplate, which was moulded to the lines of his body and followed the outlines of the abdomen. This breastplate could be embossed with Medusa's head, or inlaid with contrasting metals. Under it, and sometimes riveted to it, was a tight leather jacket. This had a skirt of one or two layers of straps which hung down to just above the knee. The straps would be coloured or gilded, and richly decorated with metal and fringe. The armour was hinged on one side and fastened by straps and buckles on the other. The helmet, which had a horsehair crest, usually dyed bright red, had flanges on either side to protect the face. These could be tied under the chin. On his legs and feet the general would wear high boots, and over the whole suit of armour he would put a cloak of any length.

Cloaks

There were several styles of cloak worn by the Romans. The abolla was similar to the Greek chlamys, though made of thicker material and usually red; the birrus was a long cloak of some heavy fabric, worn as a warm winter covering; the paludamentum and the lacerna were both like the chlamys but with minor variations; and the laena was a thick, shaggy woollen cloak, worn for warmth and protection.

The Imperial Eagle standard

Officer's bronze helmet with red plumes

Hair

Generally speaking, men wore their hair quite short, and either let it lie flat on the head or curled it with tongs. Only in times of national calamity or personal grief was it allowed to grow longer. The fashion for shaving, introduced into Greece by Alexander in about 330 B C, was followed in Rome. Women wore their hair plaited, curled, crimped and waved. One extraordinary style which appeared towards the end of the Empire was to have a pile of stiff curls supported at the front of the head by a frame or pad, with the rest of the hair coiled tightly at the back of the head.

Footwear

Unlike the Greeks, the Romans did not care to go around in bare feet, and it was considered positively bad form to do so in the house. The simple Greek sandals were thought to be unpatriotic, and the more elaborate Etruscan style was common, with a leather sole and straps over the instep and round the heel. Leather slippers, sometimes coloured or ornamented, were worn indoors. The poorer classes favoured a high felt slipper which reached partway up the leg and looked like a very thick sock. The calceus was a low boot with long straps fastened at the back which were wound round the legs just above the boot and tied in front. Senators and magistrates wore boots of red leather. Women wore boots of the same shape, but in different colours—often white—and sometimes with ribbons replacing the straps for tying the boots on.

Lady's jewellery and hairstyle

Pearl and stone earings

Gold necklaces with stones

Roman general's armour and red military cloak

Officer's leather boot

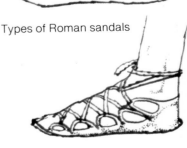

Types of Roman sandals

tong curled hair

red decorations

toga of the late Empire

yellow veil

tunic

gold bracelet

papyrus scroll

overdress

decorated stripes

calcei sandals

Roman couple

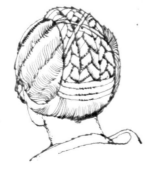

Lady's plaited hairstyle

We are captivated by dress; all is concealed by gems and gold; a woman is the least part of herself.

Ovid (c. 1 BC)

Plaited hair arrangement

Byzantine
400–900

Byzantine embroidered
trousers, worn with
tunic and cape

As the Roman Empire declined at the beginning of the fifth century, the centre of fashion moved to Byzantium (Constantinople). Many of the Roman styles, and a good deal of Roman taste for luxury and extravagance, were adapted to suit the semi-Oriental Byzantine way of life.

One of the most famous rulers of the time was the Empress Theodora, a beautiful woman who started life as the daughter of a bear feeder. She became celebrated as a dancer and a courtesan and then caught the eye of the Emperor Justinian, who changed the laws in order to marry her. Theodora has been pictured wearing lavishly embroidered, heavy silk robes encrusted with jewels, and a crown of gold, pearls and emeralds.

Byzantine styles had considerable effect on the clothes of other countries, in particular those of Russia. Byzantine designs appeared in the state dress of the Imperial Court right up to the time of the Revolution.

There are no known representations of ordinary people from Byzantine times, but it is safe to assume that they wore rather less luxurious versions of the clothes in which the rich were painted.

The well-to-do man would first put on a pair of hose. These might have been knitted, like stockings, or cut to fit from cloth or silk, and tailored to the shape of the leg. Although there is no way of proving it, hose were probably gartered. Short breeches covered the top of the stockings.

Both men and women wore an undershirt of silk, which had long, tight sleeves. The custom that had prevailed in Greek and Roman times of leaving the arms bare had finally disappeared.

On top of the shirt a man would wear a tunic, which covered the breeches. It was similar to the Roman one, varying in length from just below the knee to just over the foot. Early in the period men wore another tunic as well, similar to the Roman dalmatica. After a time this became recognized as the preserve of kings and priests.

A popular piece of jewellery was a gold collar, similar to the collar worn by the Ancient Egyptians, though a little narrower. Theodora is pictured wearing such a collar. Square and round emeralds surrounded by pearls are set all round the collar. Enormous tear-shaped pearls hang from the edge. The Empress is wearing a crown of the same design, with three long ropes of pearls falling from it onto her shoulders on each side.

Gold set with precious stones was the favourite for jewellery. Emeralds and sapphires were most frequently used, also rubies and diamonds. The stones were polished, as the art of stone-cutting had not yet been discovered.

Another fashion was the wearing of mosaic work. Designs were made up of tiny pieces of semi-precious stones, usually garnets, glass jewels and paste.

Women wore earrings, often very large ones, and gold bracelets or strings of pearls wound around their arms.

A reliquary became a fashionable item of jewellery. This was a gold cross, worn as an amulet or charm, often set with jewels or pearls, or decorated with intricate patterns in gold wire. These crosses sometimes had tiny square boxes built into the centre to hold a relic of a saint: a tooth, a hair, a nail, or even a piece of the True Cross.

Dalmatica and cloak
of learned men

Courtiers in tunics and cloaks
with tablion decorations

Empress's headdress of pearls and precious stones

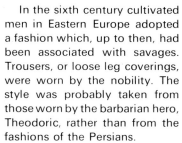

Man wearing patterned cloak and soft cap

Empress's collar, diadem and brooch

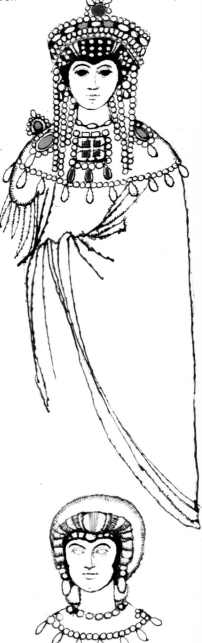

In the sixth century cultivated men in Eastern Europe adopted a fashion which, up to then, had been associated with savages. Trousers, or loose leg coverings, were worn by the nobility. The style was probably taken from those worn by the barbarian hero, Theodoric, rather than from the fashions of the Persians.

An imperial bodyguard was recruited from Scandanavia towards the end of the tenth century. These men, the Varangian Guard, wore clothes which we now associate with the Vikings.

Cloaks were worn both indoors and out. For daily wear the rectangular piece of material, familiar from earlier times, was considered enough. For more formal occasions a new shape came into being—a semi-circular cape which is still seen in the modern ecclesiastical cope.

A man's shoes would be of soft leather or fabric, without heels and cut to the shape of the foot. Very often they were embroidered, or covered with gold net sewn with pearls or other jewels. In bad weather a wealthy man might even wear a long cloak with a hood, either sewn up the front or left open and equipped

with clasps.

Rich Byzantine women had a reputation for great beauty, and the first beauty contests are supposed to have taken place in Constantinople, when the Empress Theodosia gathered together twelve of the loveliest girls in the Empire so that her son could choose a bride.

Women in and around the court, and the wives of rich merchants, dressed every bit as luxuriously as the men. Their hair was arranged very much in the way of the women of Imperial Rome, with the stiff pile of curls on top of the head. Another style was of coiled braids of hair, entwined with ropes of pearls. The braids were held together by thin ivory or metal hairpins, with carved, ornamental heads, not unlike those used by the Greeks. Sometimes a kind of turban was also worn, with the material wrapped several times around the head, often decorated with pearls or precious stones.

Women wore three or four garments. The silk or fine linen undershirt, with long, tight sleeves and a high neck, was worn under a full length tunic. They then put on a version of the

Roman stola, which was belted around the waist. Finally came the Roman palla. This garment had been unfashionable for some years when the dalmatica was the popular wear in Rome, but it now took on a new lease of life in Byzantium. In later years the stola was left off and a semi-circular cape was worn over the tunic. Women would fix the cloak with a clasp on one shoulder rather than pinning it in the centre.

Everyone, including the Imperial Guard, wore a short tunic. Over this the guardsmen wore another tunic in leather. On top was worn a coat of mail made from metal rings or discs, fastened together to form a mesh, and ornamented with large, round, patterned metal brooches. The men wore long, rather loose trousers, which were cross-gartered from the ankle to the top of the leg. A large fur cloak hung from the shoulders. Their iron helmets were decorated with large bull's horns. A long sword, hung on a leather sword belt, was slung over the right shoulder and they carried a spear with an iron head, which was often inlaid with gold and silver.

Roman hairstyle with pearl decoration

from letf to right

Empress Theodora wearing tunic, embroidered cloak, jewelled collar and diadem

Court lady wearing long tunic and woven shawl

Emperor's bodyguard in armour, with cloak and horned helmet

Materials

Clothes for the prosperous were made of almost overpoweringly rich materials. A very heavy silk called samite was used, and this could be embroidered in gold or sewn with jewels or gold pieces. Gold was beaten into flat strips, and these strips were woven into fabrics. Very fine silk was used for veils. Linen, wool and cotton were also made into various garments, the delicacy of the fabric being dictated by the amount of money the wearer could afford to spend.

Woven fabric from a Byzantine dress

Colours

It is difficult to judge the colours of the clothes worn by ordinary people since there are no representations of them in the mosaics, which are our chief source of information about Byzantine dress. Gold was certainly the most important colour for the rich, and many other deep hues were popular. Green, brown, plum, red and black can all be seen in the mosaics at Ravenna.

Shoes and Footwear

The early Byzantine shoes were not much more than elaborate versions of Roman sandals, often made of very fine leather lined with silk. Later, a definite shoe appeared, of leather or material, fastened by a jewelled clasp at the ankle. There is a picture of a tenth-century emperor wearing a high boot of red leather, cut and shaped down one side and embroidered with pearls.

The Tablion

When kings wore a rectangular cloak, somewhat like the Roman paludamentum, the front and back edges would be ornamented with a square or oblong panel of immensely rich embroidery called a tablion. The cloak itself was often covered with designs in gold, and woven with jewels and pearls. No matter how elaborate the cloak was, the tablion was even more luxurious. The emperor's cloak was always purple, a colour forbidden to anyone else except, later, the empress.

Hair and Beards

Men's hair was usually quite short, cut with a fringe, and with enough hair to rest on the nape of the neck. Beards and moustaches were not fashionable at first, though Constantine IV had a youthful beard when he arrived in Byzantium on his accession. After AD 900 most men had grown some sort of facial hair.

The Lorum

Between the eighth and twelfth centuries the Roman toga picta, which had been worn by the consuls, became a formal scarf. It was long and narrow and was draped round the body like a toga, but had only symbolic importance. The lorum was either of cloth, of gold or of heavy silk, covered in gold embroidery and sewn with jewels and pearls.

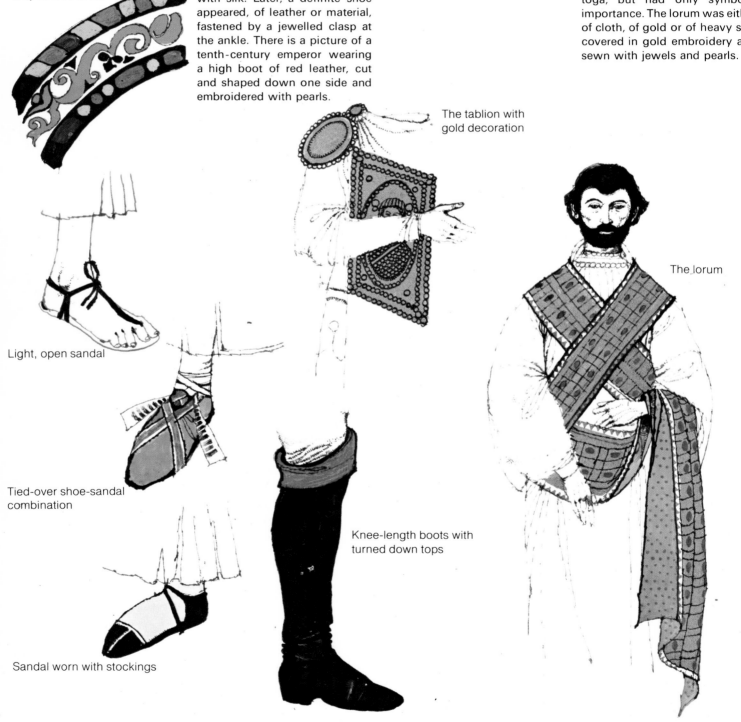

Light, open sandal

Tied-over shoe-sandal combination

Sandal worn with stockings

The tablion with gold decoration

Knee-length boots with turned down tops

The lorum

pearl earrings

necklace of precious stones

handwritten, leather bound book
with stone decorations

gold fastening brooch

pearl bracelet

tassels

patterned shawl

tablion

short tunic

embroidered
decoration

long tunic embroidered
with floral decoration

stockings

long cloak

soft leather shoes

soft leather shoes

**What is expensive for the back; what
is reasonable for the stomach.**

Babylonian Talmud (c. AD 450)

Romanesque

Priest wearing tunic and cloak
Ireland c. 890

Representations of Western dress before AD 900 are rare. It is difficult, therefore, to describe the clothes worn by Europeans during the Dark Ages. Church building increased after that date, and church sculptures show that the styles resembled those worn in the East, though they were much less magnificent. These styles were gradually adapted to the different climate and way of life in the West, and an individual look emerged during the tenth century.

The main source of influence came from France. There was obviously a good deal of difference between the cultivated Norman ways and those of the people whom they conquered.

A garment worn by men and women alike, though it varied in length and in the amount of material used, was called the bliaut. It was a tight-fitting tunic, which was laced up one or both sides. The sleeves, open below the elbow, showed the sleeve of the chemise underneath. Most men wore a bliaut that finished just below the knee. Women wore their bliaut, or dress, right to the ground, with a good deal of material in the skirt.

In the twelfth century a woman would first put on her fine chemise—sleeveless if the sleeves of her bliaut were tight, or with tight, laced sleeves if she intended them to show. On top of the chemise went the bliaut, which was tightly laced to achieve a fashionably small waist. Originally, fairly substantial material was used that would withstand the strain of the very tight lacing. In later years, when lighter materials became popular, a small waist was achieved with a corset over the chemise. This was a casing of leather or strong cloth, boned with wood or metal.

Worn loosely around the waist was a girdle made of strands of gold or silver cord, coloured wool, or strips of plaited cloth. It was held together at intervals by metal ornaments, sometimes set with jewels and occasionally decorated with enamel.

A great deal of material went into the skirt. Some very fashion-conscious ladies would wear their long skirts slit up each side, with the back allowed to form a train. The front was sometimes tied in a knot, revealing the legs, covered in loose stockings. This, however, was considered very improper, and a bit ridiculous. Another exaggeration was to use so much material in the sleeves and the ends of the veil that large knots had to be tied in them.

Conventionally dressed women often wore their long hair arranged in two long plaits, worn over the shoulders and sometimes falling to the knee. There is some evidence that long plaits were made from false hair when necessary. The plaits were braided with ribbon. The head was then covered with a light veil, which might be held in place by a circlet of gold, or perhaps a little crown of real flowers.

Women wore mantles which were usually made from semi-circular pieces of cloth, and sometimes richly embroidered. These were often handed down from generation to generation, for the quality of the material gave the garment great value.

The middle of the eleventh century saw the introduction of the shirt as an undergarment for men. Called a sherte, it was usually made of a finely woven linen called chainsil. It reached to the knee and was cut up each side, and sometimes up the front and back. Its long sleeves might have coloured embroidery at the cuffs to match the embroidery around the neck edge.

Norman warrior in mail shirt—
slit in front—and helmet c. 1150

Official in short tunic and hose

Long cloak over bliaut with
elongated point on hood c. 1200

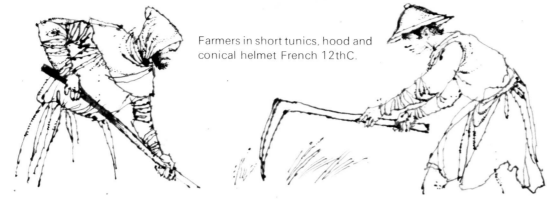
Farmers in short tunics, hood and conical helmet French 12thC.

In cold weather an additional garment could be worn over the sherte. This was cut on the same lines as the sherte but made of warmer material, and sometimes had no sleeves.

In an age of superstition one of the ways for a man to ward off an evil spell cast on his marriage was to wear his two shertes inside out at his wedding.

A man's bliaut would have the same tight bodice as a woman's. There is good reason to believe that men were not above wearing a form of corset to enhance their shape. Men wore the skirt of the bliaut shorter than a woman's. It hung in folds from the waist to below the calf. As the way the skirt hung was considered to be of great importance, a band of heavy embroidery was sewn around the edge of the skirt to help the folds hang nicely.

Men would also wear mantles, some of them of great magnificence. Mantles had a certain symbolic importance: throwing them to the ground was a form of challenge, and there is mention of both men and women doing this. The lord of a castle would present his mantle to a troubadour after an evening's

entertainment. This was likely to be his only payment, and after departing he would sell the mantle to the highest bidder.

At this time in history more attention was paid to underwear than previously, and men wore breeches under their tunics. These were made in a strange way which can still be found in parts of the world. They looked not unlike a baby's napkin, with the material wound around the waist and the back part drawn between the legs and tucked into the belt in front.

Stockings were important for everyone, from clumsy, wrinkled hose in heavy cloth to the neatly tailored silk or fine wool of the nobleman. The loose stockings had to be cross-gartered all the way up the legs, but the finer ones could be gartered at the thigh. There are a number of pictures in the Bayeux Tapestry showing what seem to be knitted, woollen stockings fastened below the knee, with the tops rolled down over the garters. This tapestry is one of the earliest sources of information about the dress of ordinary people.

In Northern Europe people dressed for warmth. Those who

could not afford the voluminous woollen garments worn by the rich would wear thick home-spun cloth. Some of it was so coarse that one could hardly tell the right side from the wrong.

A peasant woman would wear a gown on lines similar to those of a richer woman's. However, it would have loose sleeves and the skirt would reach only to the ankles. Sometimes, to achieve the same effect as embroidery used by the rich, a band of contrasting material was sewn around the cuffs as decoration.

A peasant might wear a knee length, tight-sleeved tunic of this material. Worn with it might be two pieces of fur or sheepskin, joined at the shoulders and belted around the waist with a leather thong. If a peasant could afford it, he would have a pair of loose trousers, or braies, but more often he would simply bind some leather strips around his legs to protect himself.

An everyday top garment was a hooded cape, which was made either out of rough fabric or perhaps some animal skin.

Lady in chemise, loose sleeved bliaut with decorated edges

Girl in virgin's crown wearing long bliaut and blue chemise

Lady in white veil from Bohemia wearing short surcoat over bliaut

Poor peasant in short coat, tunic and coarse leggings

Baby in swaddling clothes 12thC.

Hairdressing

In the days of William of Normandy there was a strange style of haircut for men. The hair was grown to medium length and brushed forward, and the back of the head was then shaved on a line level with the tops of the ears. Later on, long hair and beards came into fashion, and they were exaggerated to such an extent that sermons were preached against the style. In the twelfth century the locks were grown long at the back, and sometimes curled with hot irons, but the forehead was either shaved or plucked.

Moustaches

The English name Algernon is derived from a style of moustache worn at the time of the Norman invasion of Britain. The sweeping locks on the upper lip were called gernons. Sir William de Percy, a friend of the Conqueror, was known as Alsgernons, because he wore this style.

Materials

Silks were imported from the East, at incalculable cost, and there are references to richly embroidered materials, and heavily patterned fabrics. Soldiers returning from the early Crusades brought some of the weaving techniques with them, so that materials such as damask and silk were manufactured in France. Velvet was known and imported into Europe by the end of the Romanesque period. More everyday clothes were made from fustian, which was a mixture of cotton and linen. Serge, homespun and russet, a coarse cloth that was often dyed brown with bark dyes, were used. Hand knitting had been known for some time, and stockings were often knitted with thick, natural wool.

Accessories

A useful accessory, which was worn by merchants, professional men and peasants, was the gipsere. This was a leather pouch that had a long strap and was worn crosswise over the body, for carrying money, letters, or, if on a hunting trip, small game.

Fur

The draughty stone castles of the eleventh and twelfth centuries made warm clothing essential, and different kinds of furs were highly prized. Cloaks made of ermine and grey squirrel were worn by the rich; rabbit and sheepskin—and sometimes even wolf—were made into protective garments for the poor.

Jewellery

The Byzantine taste for jewellery was not transferred to Europe, though such ornament as was worn was often copied from Eastern originals. As the head was usually covered, there was no space for earrings, and bracelets were out of place on tightly sleeved arms. An important item of jewellery was the brooch, used for fastening cloaks, for clasping the neck of the tunic or gown, or for decorating the waist-girdle. These brooches, known as agrafes, were in gold set with pearls or uncut precious stones, or decorated with enamel. The gold and enamel work of Limoges was particularly sought after.

Shoes

Although shoes for ordinary wear followed traditional patterns, being cut from cloth or leather to the shape of the foot, some very peculiar designs could be seen. These were derived from those of Count Fulk of Anjou, who had such disfigured feet that his shoes were made very long, with pointed toes, to hide the deformities. Someone had the idea of stuffing the points of the shoes with tow, and shoemakers carried the idea a step further by shaping the points like scorpions' or serpents' tails.

Early Norman hairstyle with Algernon moustaches

Later hairstyle 12thC.

Norman soldier in armour—helmet, hauberk with short sleeves, and with bound arms

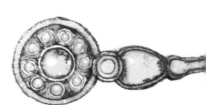

Lombardic cloak clasp in gold c. 900

Pointed shoe

stiffened white headdress

Norman Nobleman and Lady

bliaut with loose sleeves, slit sides

wool cloak with gold brooch

embroidered wool girdle

decorated sword be

knightly sword

long tunic
embroidered edges

woollen hose

chemise

soft leather shoes

Romanesque decoration from Ireland

Rich silks of Zazamanc, as green as any grass, and of Araby, white as the snow, were now inlaid with precious stones, to make clothing of high quality.

The Nibelungenlied (c. AD 1200 trans. D G Mowatt)

Royal Crown of St Stephen 10thC.

Early Gothic 1200–1350

Long tunic with hose

Louis IX of France, born in 1215, reigned from age eleven for the next forty-four years. He was a very religious man, who set an example for France, and the rest of the fashionable world, with his taste for simplicity and dislike of extravagance. He was enormously popular with the Court and his subjects. He married Margaret of Provence, sister to the Queen of England. His preference for plainness and restraint was, therefore, copied in the Courts of Europe. The exaggerated styles which had been popular in the previous century were replaced by nobler, dignified clothes, with the accent on richness of material and contrast of colours.

Most pictures of this time show men wearing what seem to be tights, but in fact their legs were covered by stockings. These were attached to the belt or to the waist of a short under-jacket by means of ties or points, as they were called. A man in the early thirteenth century wore a linen undershirt and a pair of linen briefs called slops. He then put on his short, sleeveless jacket and his hose. On top of them he wore a calf length tunic

in some soft material. Finally, he wore the latest French fashion garment, the cyclas. This was also calf length, without sleeves so that the sleeves of the tunic would show. The cyclas could be belted or not, as the wearer thought fit. Though simple in line, it was often of very rich or embroidered material.

Towards the end of the century a new garment appeared for both men and women, though of differing cut and length—short for the men. This was the cotehardie, a tightly fitting tunic, made in four parts and seamed up the front, back and each side. Very often the panels of material were chosen in contrasting colours. These could be repeated in the hose, which would be cut and sewn to echo the "parti-colouring" of the stylish new tunic.

The short, sleeveless coat under the cotehardie was often padded in the chest to give the wearer a handsome figure. It is thought that men could have padded hose made as well, if their legs were too thin.

Yet another garment which could be worn over the cote-hardie was a calf length robe,

called a surcote or pelicon. It had a round neck and full sleeves, under which the tight sleeves of the cotehardie could be seen. The surcote would be made of some rich material, and lined with a contrasting colour, or sometimes fully lined with fur.

The most usual item of head-gear was the coif—a white, close-fitting cap of linen, cotton or silk, which tied under the chin. It was worn indoors as well as outside, and very often was worn with another hat or hood on top of it. The hood was conical, with a hole for the face to show through, and a good deal of fullness of material that would rest on the shoulders.

Towards the end of the thirteenth century the point of the hood, which was known as the liripipe, grew longer and longer. A fashionable young man would think nothing of a liripipe two metres long. One day a court dandy completely altered the look of his hood by putting the hole for his face on top of his head. The wide part of the cone hung down one side and the liripipe the other. What then became the brim of the hat was turned up. The full material could

The cyclas and a coif cap

Nobleman in parti-coloured dress, with tall hat, sword belt and sword

Peasant wearing straw hat over coi[f] loose tunic showing slops, and sto[ckings]

Man's hat over coif

Lady's coif

Man's hood with long liripipe

be tucked into the brim, giving a coxcomb effect. The long liripipe was worn hung over one arm, or tucked into the wearer's belt at the waist.

Shoes were very plain in shape, though often made from rich or embroidered materials: silk, velvet or leather. There are pictures of men wearing black, knee length boots, which fitted the leg closely and tied with a strap under the knee. These boots would have been in cloth or leather.

Women wore an undergown with tight, long sleeves and a full length skirt. This garment would have been made in a very rich material. Over it was worn another gown, with elbow length sleeves and a low, round neck. The skirt of the top gown was often extremely long, forming a train at the back, and had to be held up in front. This was not only to keep it from under the wearer's feet, but also to show off the skirt of the expensive undergown.

A woman's neck was very often covered. One method of doing this was to take a piece of fine linen and wrap it round the neck in loose folds, so that

the neckline of the gown covered one edge of it. The sides of the other edge were drawn up over elaborate coils of hair on the side of the head, and pinned over the coils. This was called the gorget. It could be worn either by itself, or with a hat or other head-covering, when it was then known as a wimple.

The woman's version of the cotehardie began as a rather more elaborate version of the undergown. It took on a shape of its own because of a fashion for a top garment which had no sleeves and cutaway sides. This revealed more of the undergown than was usual, and for a time the top garment was dispensed with completely. The rich flowing undergown had a tight bodice and sleeves. Two pockets, perpendicular openings, were placed in the front of the skirt for the fashionable to put their hands, in order to lift the skirt off the ground. The cotehardie was either laced up the back or buttoned up the front. The sleeves often closed with long rows of buttons, and could also have pieces of gauzy fabric trailing from the elbow.

There was a much greater

variety of materials to choose from by the thirteenth century. Many of them were still imported from the Middle and Far East: camelot, which was like a fine cashmere, made in Asia from camel's hair; and tartaire, a kind of silk, originally made in Tartary, but later copied by Western weavers. Other fabrics came from cotton grown in Italy and woven in France; from Flanders, which produced a very fine, almost cobweb-like woollen cloth called lyraigne; and from Liège, where they made a fine linen material known as cloth of lake. Some of the rougher materials had suitably down-to-earth names. Carry-marry was a rough serge cloth. Linsey woolsey was a homespun mixture of linen and wool imported from Florence.

There was a much greater range of colours, and expensive fabrics were often very bright, with red, blue and green predominating. Ordinary people wore dull greens and browns, as well as the yellows, oranges and violets which could be achieved by herb and bark dyes. There seems to have been a fashion at the time for bright red undergarments.

Lady's dress with tight, tailored bodice
Crespine headdres, draped with veil

Married lady with kerchief, undergown and loose surcoat

Young lady wearing garland, undertunic and surcoat

Old pilgrim woman in old-fashioned cloth headdress and loose dress

Heraldry

Between 1216 and 1270 there were four Crusades to the Holy Land, led by the kings of France, England and Germany. It was during these Crusades that the traditions of heraldry were formed. Originally, the simplest way to ensure that a knight in armour was recognisable on the battlefield was to allow him to wear a distinguishing badge on the linen surcoat which he wore over his armour. The Knights Templar wore a red cross, and the Knights of St John a Maltese cross. Gradually these identifying signs became more complicated, as knights began to wear badges associated with their families. These might be animals, or stars, or towers, and as one family married into another the badges would be shown together.

Armour

Knights wore chain-mail, with a tunic which reached to the knees, hose and a hood. About 1300 they began to add plate armour, beginning with shaped and jointed plates which were strapped on to the front of the leg to protect the legs and feet. They also wore steel helmets, with hinged face-coverings or visors with openings for breathing and seeing. A popular garment for wearing under the chain-mail was the hauqueton, a padded jacket made out of coarse cotton, which was almost impenetrable. Some foot soldiers wore it without any mail covering.

Heavy helmet
with bird decoration

Pilgrims' Signs

In the twelfth century people would make pilgrimages to the Holy Land and, on their return, would fix a scallop shell in their hats as a sign that they had completed their journey. This practice spread in the thirteenth century, when travellers visited shrines of famous saints all over Europe. They would take care to collect a badge associated with the particular saint of their pilgrimage. These little signs were made in brass, lead or pewter, with pins for fastening them to the clothes, or with holes so that they could be sewn on permanently.

Jewellery

Probably because of the amount of covering that went on the neck and arms, necklaces and bracelets do not seem to have had much place at this time. Rings were worn. Brooches were used by men and women to fasten cloaks, and men sometimes wore them to decorate their hats. These brooches were round or oval, and were fine examples of the goldsmith's art.

Accessories

Gloves were worn much more frequently at this time, either rough mittens for work in the fields, or strong, well-cut gauntlets for riding and hawking. Most people wore a purse hanging from the belt, and men would carry their daggers pushed through the strap of the purse. A housewife might carry useful objects around with her hanging from her belt—a sewing kit or a set of keys, or a cooking knife.

Hair and Headdresses

Long hair was still fashionable for women, and it was usually done in long plaits, which were sometimes intertwined with ribbon or gold braid. These plaits could be put up in a number of ways, the most popular of which was the ramshorn, where the plaits were brought round from the back and twisted into coils over the ears. Sometimes a long piece of silk was used to cover the back of the head and the plaits, and was wound into coils. This formed a headdress in its own right. A band of linen, called a barbette, was frequently worn, placed under the chin with the ends meeting on top of the head. The hair might be encased in a net of gold braid, called a crispine. A shallow pill-box hat, the female version of the coif, was one of the most usual head coverings for women.

Knight Templar with Templar cross in non-military headgear

Knight in chain armour wearing the Maltese cross

Lady's "pork pie" coif

Gothic fibula in gold
and precious stones

"pork pie" coif

Heavy decorated helmet

undergown with
tight-fitting sleeves

heavy chainmail

sword and
sword belt

surcoat with coat of arm

sleeveless surcoat

spurs with straps

Decorated helmet

The cook bigan of him to rewe
And bought him clothes all spannewe;
He bought him both hosen and shon,
And sone dide him dones on.
When he was clothed, hosed, and shod,
Was non so fair under God.

Havelok the Dane (c. 1275)

Decoration from contemporary manuscript

33

Late Gothic 1350–1450

Knight's tournament helmet

Daily life became easier in the late fourteenth century. Leisure increased and this, combined with wealth, gave people more time for living and dressing. At the same time, terrible plagues ravaged the countries of Europe. The wealth of large families passed into a few hands and resulted in a worldly, luxurious outlook with regard to clothing.

Men's clothes became more carefully tailored, and the basic garments fitted the figure much more closely. Stockings gradually turned into what we now think of as tights, and were attached by ties, or points, to a very short sleeveless jacket. On top of this jacket a man would wear a *jupon,* or *pourpoint,* a jacket with either tight or loose sleeves, depending on the wearer's taste. It was characterized by, and criticized for, its shortness. In France, contemporary writers even blamed the loss of the battle of Crécy on the shortness of the jupon, saying that it was so indecent that, "Anyone standing behind them could see their hose as well as the anatomy beneath." The cotehardie of earlier years grew shorter and was richly embroid-ered with gold thread and jewels. It became a symbol of the aristocracy.

A garment which made its first appearance at this time was the houppelande, a floor length gown with enormous sleeves. The name derives from *hopa,* the Spanish word for a long gown with sleeves. This robe began as a fashionable innovation for the young men about the court. It soon became everyday wear for anyone who had any pretensions to modishness. It could be made in one piece, with a small, buttoned opening for the head; or open right up the front, and then buttoned; or with two slits up the sides. It was always belted. Its two characteristics were huge sleeves and a stand-up collar. The full sleeves were cut round the edges in fantastic shapes known as dagging. Each section of the dagging was trimmed with jewels and embroidery, with personal initials, or coronets, or love-knots. The decoration told the wearer's rank or affections. Usually the houppelande was so long that it trailed on the ground.

There were, however, more practical versions of the garment. One, the "bastard" houppelande, fell to just below the calves, and made up for lack of length with additional dagging and decoration. The riding version of the gown was open up the front and the back, for convenience when sitting on a horse.

Another of the fashion introductions of the period was the very high collar. This was either part of the houppelande or could be attached to the cotehardie. These collars stood well up at the back. They could be buttoned up tight under the chin or cut away in front, leaving the throat bare. Sometimes the back was so exaggerated that the top of the collar reached well up the back of the head, and had to be stiffened with whalebone.

Men wore calf length, soft leather boots outdoors. For riding, longer boots were pulled up over the knees. The boots were fitted to the leg, and were sometimes so pliable that they needed no fastening at all. There are, however, examples of boots which were laced up the inside leg, or buckled up the sides. Indoors, men wore soft shoes of

Furlined coat and fur hat for riding c. 1430

Houppelande with turban like hat made from long liripipe

Lady in elaborate hairstyle—houppelande dress, chemise

Soldier with longbow—padded jupon, hat and tight hose

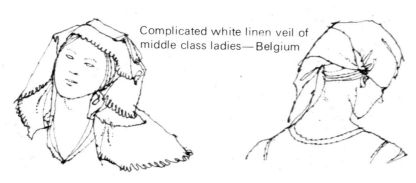
Complicated white linen veil of middle class ladies—Belgium

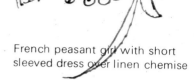
Lady's dress decorated with bells—Germany

French peasant girl with short sleeved dress over linen chemise

Starched linen headdress (left), steeple shaped hennin with flowing veil (right)

leather, cloth, velvet or felt. For a short time there was a fashion for elongating the toes of the shoes, and stiffening the points with wire or whalebone. This fashion was carried to ridiculous lengths by some young dandies, whose shoes had such long points that they had to be attached to their knees with fine chains.

Women at this time wore, first of all, a chemise of silk or fine linen. Over it was worn a tight fitting bodice and full skirt, cut together in one piece. Known as a corset, it had long, tight sleeves, and usually laced up the front. Over the corset a woman wore a surcote with a deep neck and very large armholes, so that the richness of the underdress might be shown off.

Women also had their own version of the houppelande, sometimes with the very high collar and sometimes with a turned-over collar like a sailor's.

The houppelande could be un-belted, in which case it would have a fairly tight bodice, or it could be worn with a high belt under the bosom. It was trimmed with fur, dagged with fanciful patterns round the edges, set with jewels, or embroidered with gold thread. Sometimes the decoration combined all four.

When it came to hats and head-dresses, women let their imagination run wild. At the French Court the ladies' head-dresses became so enormous that the architects of the Castle of Blois were obliged to enlarge the door openings. The nets of gold braid, the crispines of the earlier century, grew into large gold mesh boxes that were worn over the ears and known as tem-plettes. These boxes were probably joined together over the top of the head, and the head was then covered with a fine lawn *couvrechef*. If the lady's rank warranted it, she might then wear a small coronet on top of the whole construction. In the early fifteenth century Marie de Clèves introduced a fashion called a hennin, which was a cone balanced on the head. It was most likely fixed in some way, perhaps with a comb to attach it to the hair. From the tip of the cone hung a light veil, sometimes woven with gold thread, and made out of gauze in brilliant colours. The fashion passed from France to Italy and Germany, and was the subject of a great deal of criticism. In Italy the priests taught little boys to run after the women in the streets shouting "hennin, hen-nin", but this had no effect on the wearers. Isabella of Bavaria is known to have worn a jewelled hennin made of gold brocade, a metre long, with a veil falling from the point and covering her shoulders and back.

Very little is known of women's shoes, as their dresses were so long that the shoes were seldom seen. It is assumed that they were similar to those worn by men. Both men and women wore high wooden pattens tied on to their shoes when they went out, to keep the mud off the delicate materials, and also to try to stop the hems of their garments from trailing in the dirt.

A strange fashion, which last-ed for about thirty years, and had its origin in Germany, was for men and women to decorate their clothes with bells. Bells were sewn on collars, on the hems of tunics, fastened to belts or even to wide bands of embroidery that were worn across the body.

Young man wearing pourpoint jacket, hose, long, pointed shoes, with hat and scarf

Padded jupon, tight hose, pointed shoes

Long, loose sleeved dresses

Accessories

Men and women both carried pomanders, hollow pierced metal balls. They contained religious relics or, more often, sponges soaked in perfume to keep away some of the more offensive smells. Another form of pomander was an orange, spiked all over with cloves and then roasted to keep its delicate scent. Men often wore an ornamental dagger called a *misericorde,* named after the dagger used by a knight to finish off a defeated adversary. Gloves were made out of kid, chamois or fabric, and were often embroidered and stitched with contrasting colours. White gloves were particularly fashionable. If the wearer wanted to show off some fine jewellery, holes could be cut in the fingers of the gloves.

Fur

One of the most fashionable furs was *menu-vair* or miniver, the fur from the belly of the grey squirrel. Obviously an enormous amount of the little pelts was necessary to make up a reasonable amount of fur and miniver was, therefore, very expensive. In spite of this it was used for trimming hats and tunics, and even for lining entire gowns. Astrakhan, a variety of lambskin, was one of the most popular cheaper furs. Ordinary people made do with fox, rabbit or muskrat. Sometimes fur could be dyed bright colours to match the garment to which it was attached.

Soldiers

There was a fashion among gentlemen for wearing pieces of armour with their civilian clothes —particularly leg-pieces, which could be shown under the slit sides of the houppelande. The ordinary soldier had to make do with a padded jupon. Over this he wore a chain-mail covering, or perhaps a *gambeson,* an over-tunic made of heavy canvas or light leather, quilted and studded with nails. His legs and feet apparently had no special protection. A chain-mail hood and a steel hat with a narrow brim completed the uniform.

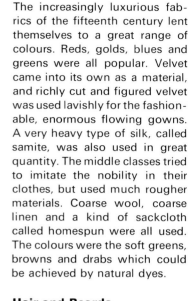

Foot soldier in padded jupon, chain-mail hood and flat steel helmet

Colours and Materials

The increasingly luxurious fabrics of the fifteenth century lent themselves to a great range of colours. Reds, golds, blues and greens were all popular. Velvet came into its own as a material, and richly cut and figured velvet was used lavishly for the fashionable, enormous flowing gowns. A very heavy type of silk, called samite, was also used in great quantity. The middle classes tried to imitate the nobility in their clothes, but used much rougher materials. Coarse wool, coarse linen and a kind of sackcloth called homespun were all used. The colours were the soft greens, browns and drabs which could be achieved by natural dyes.

Hair and Beards

Women's hair, though carefully plaited and coiled, was generally hidden under elaborate headdresses. Men were content with a very simple hair style to begin with, parted in the middle and cut off at about chin level. A French style introduced smooth, oiled hair with the ends rolled round a pad of material. A feather decoration could be worn in the middle of the brow. Beards and moustaches seem to have been a matter of personal taste. Older men would wear them, while younger preferred to be clean-shaven. It is said that Edward II, who was clean-shaven, was obliged to shave in cold, muddy water when he was imprisoned, but insisted on shaving nevertheless.

Cosmetics

Women plucked the hair on their foreheads. They plucked their eyebrows to a fine line or even completely, so that artificial eyebrows could be painted on a little higher. They painted their faces, washed their hair once a week and followed recipes for making the hair blonde with applications of henna, gorse flowers, saffron, eggs or calves' kidneys. They put honey on their lips to make them firm, and rinsed their mouths with sweet wine to keep their gums healthy.

White, lady's glove and pomander ball.

Hennin with light veil

Long houppelande gown in green samite with embroidery

Red gown with miniver pelt lining in decorative pattern

hat with long liripipe

bleached blonde hair
later hairstyle

plucked eyebrows

fashionable makeup

high collar

brocaded houppelande

long houppelande type gown
c. 1410

wide hip belt

g sleeves

silk chemise

Horned headdress c. 1410

There is no new guise that is not old.

Chaucer: The Knight's Tale (c. 1386)

Misericorde dagger with gold
mounts

The Italian Renaissance

Cap with dagging

Young man in tight
hose and cod piece,
padded jerkin with
wide sleeves, cap

In the middle of the fifteenth century Italy, ideally placed between the West and the newly discovered East, sent merchant ships all over the known world. The wealthy merchants patronized such artists as Leonardo da Vinci, Botticelli, Michelangelo and Titian. The Medici and Borgia families flourished at this time, as did the legendary statesman, Niccolo Machiavelli. A new age of artistic achievement, of interest in music and painting, had been emerging slowly during the previous hundred years. It now appeared in full in cities like Florence, Venice, Rome, Naples and Mantua.

The fashionable people in many countries did their best to distort the outlines of their bodies by padding their clothes whereever possible. The Italians, however, preferred comparative simplicity. The exaggerated clothes worn by the Germans and the Dutch would have been too hot, in any case, for the Mediterranean climate.

Men wore a tight fitting basic outfit which consisted of hose, often visible right to the waist, and a shirt which could be of linen but might equally well be of silk or shot taffeta. Taffeta was recommended as a good lining material for discouraging fleas. Shirts could be white or coloured. They might be embroidered round the cuffs with stitching in a contrasting colour.

The hose could still be cut from material, but were more usually knitted, and were hardly ever in a plain colour. All kinds of variations were common: one leg checked while the other was striped, patterns which changed at the knee, or patches of different colours on the thigh or the calf. Sometimes each leg was divided lengthwise in a number of contrasting colours.

The brevity of the upper garments led to the introduction of the cod-piece, a pouch made of the same material as the hose and fastened over the crutch with ties or buckles.

About 1500, a new type of leg covering appeared: ''upper stocks'', for the top of the leg, almost like tight trunks; and ''lower stocks'', for the lower leg. Garters were necessary to keep the lower stocks smooth, and these could be jewelled or embroidered.

A doublet, which developed from the jacket of earlier years, was worn over the shirt. The doublet was similar to the modern waistcoat, and finished at the waist. Full length hose were attached to it with points, or ties. It could be sleeveless, or with sleeves that were attached to the armholes with ties. The front part of the doublet and the lower part of the sleeve would show under the jerkin.

The jerkin was usually open down the front, and had a knee length skirt. Younger men wore a much shorter skirt. The longer skirt was made with unpressed pleats. The jerkin was belted either with a metal belt or with a silk sash or ribbon. Its sleeves and hem would often be trimmed with fur. If it was worn open, to show the doublet underneath, the jerkin might have a wide fur collar with revers.

Another style of tunic was closed right up the front to a high roll collar. It had wide, open sleeves which showed the full length of the doublet sleeves underneath. A third variation is shown on a Florentine wedding *cassone*. It depicts a short, richly patterned doublet with a high neck and puffed sleeves, worn

Doublet with attached sleeves,
loose shirt, hose

Youth in doublet, hose and upper
stocks and cod piece

Elder Statesman wearing flat
velvet cap, fur trimmed gown.
Venetian 1590

Side view of shoe and platform

Venetian high heeled, platform shoes 16thC.

Hair decorated with ribbons and jewels, shaved forehead

under a sleeveless, knee length tabard, open up both sides.

Men's hats took on a variety of shapes. The simplest was a plain, brimless cap, which could be trimmed with gold braid round the edge, and decorated with a jewelled brooch or feather. A Spanish fashion, adopted by several other countries, was a tall velvet cap with six or seven sides. A round hat with deep fringe round the brim originated in Portugal. One of the most usual Italian styles, however, was a plain hat with a domed crown of medium height. The little brim turned up at the back and came to a point in the front. The small feathers which decorated men's hats in the last quarter of the fifteenth century gave way to larger ones from swans and peacocks. These, in turn, were replaced by ostrich plumes.

Young men wore short cloaks outdoors. These were usually cut in one semi-circular piece and trimmed with fur and jewels. Older men preferred ankle length gowns. A symbol of authority in Venice was the toga. It bore no resemblance to the Roman garment, but was simply a flowing gown with loose sleeves and a

band of colour round the edge: black for the nobility and magistrates, purple for senators and violet for scholars.

Italian women of the Renaissance did not care for the elaborate, all-concealing headdresses that were worn elsewhere. They wore their hair completely or partly displayed. Even if they wore hats, the hair would show underneath. It might be pulled through the open crown of a hat and arranged with ribbons or gold net.

At the beginning of the Renaissance, dresses were similar in style to earlier ones, though the exaggeratedly long skirts had been shortened. In the early fifteen hundreds a new style emerged, and a chemise of silk or fine linen, with a high neck, was worn underneath. The new dress style had a low, square neckline and huge puffed sleeves. The full, floor length skirt was attached to a tight, boned bodice, and could be caught up on one side to give a glimpse of the rich petticoat underneath. The sleeves were either of patterned material, which contrasted with the rest of the dress, or else heavily embroidered or jewelled. Some-

times the chemise was not worn and the bare shoulders were then covered with a wide silk mesh that was joined with jewels or gold beads.

The wooden pattens, which women had worn earlier to keep the mud off their delicate shoes, now became much more elaborate. They were eventually worn as shoes in their own right, with embroidered brocade uppers. The brocade-covered wooden or cork soles were sometimes as much as six inches high. The fashion was carried to such an extreme that some ladies had to be supported by a maid on each side when they went out walking.

Both women and men usually slept naked. During the fifteenth century, however, women began to wear night-shifts of fine linen or silk. These garments became very magnificent. Lucrezia Borgia owned two hundred, and one Venetian beauty owned fifty plain ones and eight decorated with gold and silk embroidery.

Many poor country people still wore the same sort of basic clothes that they had worn for the past hundred years, but prosperous peasants wore rough versions of fashionable styles.

Venetian lady with turban hairstyle, tight waisted dress

Low cut dress with attached sleeves, slit to show embroidered underskirt, chemise—Venice

Embroidered dress, attached and slashed sleeves—Florence

Peasant in doublet, loose shirt, unattached hose

Hair and Beards

Blonde hair was very fashionable and women would spend hours bleaching, burnishing and frizzing their hair into the popular shapes. Unmarried girls wore their hair long, while older or married women could choose from a great number of different styles. Young men also wore their hair long, a fashion that was frowned upon by some members of the clergy. Men were generally clean-shaven. Those who did wear beards, however, had a variety of shapes to choose from: pointed, or brush-shaped, or even forked. Some true eccentrics even had one side of the beard shorter than the other. The beards and hairstyles could be kept in shape by the use of resin or egg white.

Armour

The centre of the armour making industry was Milan, and the trade was dominated by the Missaglia family. As guns came to be used in battle, armour became less prized for its protective qualities than for its decoration and elegance. It was worn on peaceful ceremonial occasions. The cuirass, made of tempered steel, was moulded to the body of the wearer. It had hip plates attached at each side, which were themselves joined to thigh pieces. These were attached to plates, and they to the greaves which covered the front of the lower leg. The armour was decorated all over with intricate designs which were either etched on to the metal, or moulded in relief. Lances, swords, daggers and crossbows were all used, and mounted knights carried shields.

Materials and Colours

The nobility wore rich silks, satins, taffetas, velvets and cloth of gold or silver. Most of the fabrics were in strong colours, and black velvet was used a great deal. As foreign travel and trade increased, so did the variety of fabrics and the means of dyeing them different colours. Plain and patterned materials were combined in both men's and women's clothes. The patterns could either be woven into the cloth or applied afterwards, in abstract designs or in the shapes of fruit, flowers or animals. Sometimes personal initials were embroidered on the fabrics, either singly or in an all over pattern.

Decorated Italian armour for parade with jointed arms, breastplate, closed helmet with visor

The Doge

Venice was ruled by the Council of Ten, at the head of which was the Duke, or Doge, who was elected by the Council and frequently deposed by them. Doge Francesco Foscari was given an annual pension of 1,500 gold ducats when he was deposed, though he only lived for a week after the event. He was lucky, since some of his predecessors had been beheaded, or blinded and exiled. For ceremonial and public occasions, the Doge wore a traditional costume which did not change in design during the centuries the office existed. It was of great splendour—a pointed cap worn over a white linen coif, and a long cape with a stand-up round collar. The main colours of this costume were red and gold, though the pattern of the fabric changed over the years. The cape was fastened down the front with enormous gold buttons. Underneath the cape, the Doge would wear garments in keeping with the time, though it is likely that they would be slightly old-fashioned.

Accessories

Handkerchiefs came back into fashion with the Renaissance. At first they were used only by the nobility, who had special laws enacted to keep handkerchiefs exclusive. Later on, however, their use became more general. Women carried handbags, which held their make-up. They carried fans—square, oblong or circular pieces of stiffened fabric attached to intricately carved or engraved handles. Small hand mirrors in similar shapes were also carried. Men had purses attached to their belts. An ornamental, but none the less lethal, dagger could be worn, pushed through the belt straps. Dress swords, lighter than those used in battle, appeared in about 1510.

Jewellery

Renaissance men in Italy seem to have been fairly restrained in their use of jewellery. Most pictures show them wearing little more than a brooch in their hats, or sometimes on their sleeves, and perhaps a gold chain round their necks. They would wear one or two rings, but earrings were not fashionable, for a young man's hair was usually worn long. Women, on the other hand, put on as much jewellery as they conveniently could. Pearls edged their necklines and gems and gold decorated their headdresses. They wore ropes of pearls round their necks and drop earrings if their ears were visible. Some of the pearls must have been false, but there is evidence that the majority of them were real. Gold linked or jewelled chain girdles were worn round the waist, and various accessories might be hung from the chains: a pomander, a pair of scissors, keys or a rosary.

Lady's plaited hairstyle late 15thC.

Man's long hairstyle with cap

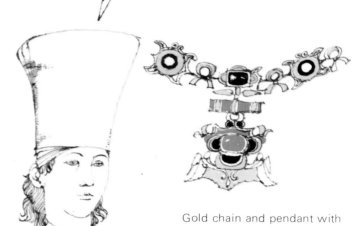

Elongated conical felt hat from Lombardy

Gold chain and pendant with stones

curled blonde hair

jewelled headband

brightly coloured cap

gold and stone necklace

fur lined coat

tabard

coat of arms inset on background

Venetian silk gown

slashed finestrella sleeves

black under tunic

flowing chemise sleeves

skirt held up for walking

tight hose

rocaded underskirt

soft leather shoes

velvet purse with metal clasp to wear on belt

Che quant' era più ornata, era più brutta—
Who seems most hideous when adorned the most.

Ariosto: Orlando Furioso (1516)

Long pointed shoe

English Tudor

Dogaline coat, oriental design buttoned caftan, gaiters

The English Tudor monarchs, Henry VII, Henry VIII and Mary, reigned from 1485 to 1558. The Renaissance was taking place in Italy during this time, and many of the ideas that were born in Florence, Venice and Rome found their way to England. This coincided with a great increase in England's prosperity, as she settled down to a time of comparative peace after the Wars of the Roses. The rich were still very rich, and the poor were still very poor; however, as in the other countries of Europe, foreign travel had opened up new markets for adventurous merchants, and a prosperous middle class began to appear.

The reign of Henry VII was a transitional period in terms of fashion, although it covered twenty-four years. Henry was a tight-fisted man and did not encourage great display at his Court. Tudor fashions as we know them are always associated with his son, Henry VIII. His portrait by Hans Holbein, the German artist, gives some idea of the splendour of the clothing of the rich. Holbein also painted portraits of five of Henry's six wives.

Generally speaking, the English styles were less graceful than the Italian ones; however, as most young men with any money used to travel on the Continent, it was not unusual to see one country's ideas appearing in the fashions of another. The Germans wore very elaborate clothes, with enormous padded shoulders and chests, huge, ungainly shoes and wide hats covered with feathers. While the English outline was based on the German one, it was done with a certain amount of restraint. Although the average courtier looked bulky, he was not altogether ungainly.

A Tudor gentleman of about 1530 wore a linen shirt and full length hose tied to a belt or a little short jacket. A pair of upper stocks were worn on top of the hose. This type of upper stocks was much looser in the leg than the Italian style. They were made out of plain material or from bands of silk, called panes, which were attached to a plain coloured base. A gentleman's doublet had enormous sleeves, padded with straw and slashed to let the material of the lining show through. If the top of the sleeve was raised high above the shoulder it was described as being mahoitred, from the French word maheutre, meaning a padded sleeve. The front of the doublet was slashed as well, and could be left partly open to show the elaborate embroidery on the shirt underneath. A gown or surcote was worn over everything else. It was sometimes sleeveless, with the armholes cut deep enough to allow the doublet sleeves to pass through. Sometimes the gown had even more enormous puffed sleeves than the doublet, which reached about half way down the arm. The top gown was usually lined with fur, and remained extremely popular until the introduction of the newest fashion from Spain, a cape. The Spanish cape, called the muceta, was almost three-quarters of a circle in shape. It first appeared in about 1556, and caught on immediately. The muceta had a large, pointed hood which fell down the back, and was trimmed with buttons. The cloak was very often lined with heavy fur, and it had a wide, fur collar, which meant that the hood was only ornamental.

Men's hair was cut short, and most men wore beards and moustaches. Their hats were

Doublet with slashed sleeves, high collar, ruff

Long skirted doublet, fur-lined gown, hose, square-toed shoes

Two ways of wearing Tudor gable coif with black coronet

Gold and jewel decorated Tudor gable coif with black coronet worn up

Lady's sleeve with chemise pulled through fastenings

usually versions of the flat cap known as the bonnet. Sometimes a jewelled band decorated the edge, and often a small feather was pinned on with a jewelled brooch.

A fashionable lady of the time wore a gown with a low, square neckline, with the ruffled edge of her chemise showing over the top. The gown was made of velvet or brocade. Sleeves were tight at the shoulder and gradually widened until they were very long and full. They were turned back to show a rich lining of fur or contrasting material, and a false undersleeve. The undersleeve was puffed out and slashed to show what was supposed to be the sleeve of the chemise. This, however, was probably some additional material. Round the wrist was a ruffle of lace.

The skirt of the gown opened right down the front to reveal an underskirt of material which matched the false sleeves. This underskirt and the large undersleeves were all that remained of the complete undergown of earlier years. As the bodice of the top gown became tighter and more boned it was uncomfortable to wear an undergown. The

bell shaped skirts were not held out by hoops, but by the quantity of material in the pleated petticoats underneath. Rich Tudor women paid a great deal of attention to their appearance. It is recorded that, even for her execution, Anne Boleyn dressed in a grey brocade dress with huge turned back sleeves, lined with grey squirrel fur, and with undersleeves and skirt of rose coloured satin.

The most typical woman's head-dress in the early part of the period was the gable or kennel shape. It began as a plain black velvet hood with an ornamented band on the front. Very soon the band was stiffened with wire and buckram and took on a gable shape. It was then made even more elaborate. A band of striped silk was worn underneath it, just showing under the gable at the front. Jewels and gold work trimmed the front. This head-dress went out of fashion when the Duchess of Suffolk introduced the horseshoe shaped French hood. The front part was again stiffened and decorated, and a band of pleated gold or white gauze trimmed the lower edge. Both these styles of head-

dress were worn over a white linen cap which was held close to the head with a linen bandage. The cap had lappets over the ears to which the long sides of the hoods were secured.

No festivity in a great house was considered complete without the presence of a fool, or "patch", whose name was taken from the Italian *pazzo*, meaning mad. The fool would wear particoloured hose like those fashionable in Italy. Over them he wore a jerkin with the sleeves and body coloured in different ways. His tabard often had sleeves which were wide at the top. He wore a three-pointed hood and often had bells sewn on to various parts of his garments.

A new class of country people emerged towards the end of the fifteenth century, consisting of those who had acquired enough money to buy the land which they farmed. These yeomen, and their wives, wore clothes made of simple materials when they went about their daily work. The styles which they chose, however, were similar to those worn by the rich.

Gentleman in late 16thC. French style doublet, breeches, and short coat, with tennis racket

Merchant's wife in starched headdress, wearing overgown held up by fastenings and belts

Boy in sleeveless gown, short doublet and long loose breeches

Gown and undergown over conical farthingale

Shoes

The typical square-toed shoes of sixteenth century England are sometimes attributed to the fact that Henry VIII had gout. As he did not start to suffer from the complaint until middle life it is more likely that the fashion started in France, where Charles VIII had special shoes designed to disguise his deformed foot. Shoes might be of leather, silk, or velvet, generally without heels. In about 1520 extra pieces of leather began to be attached to the toes and heels of flat shoes, paving the way for the formal heel. Quite often the sole of the shoe was made of leather or cork and was a different colour from the upper. Sometimes there was a layer of cork between the upper and the leather sole, giving the wearer a little extra height.

Square-toed shoes with slashing

Padded codpiece

The Cod-piece

The simple cod-piece, or pouch, of the Italian Renaissance was designed to give a semblance of decency to the fashionable tight hose and extra-short jackets. It was exaggerated first by the Germans and then by the English into a vast, padded, embroidered and jewelled addition to formal costume. It seems to have served no useful purpose except to draw attention to the wearer's masculinity. Sometimes it was used as a purse.

Slashing

This fashion was carried to extreme lengths by the Germans and was almost as popular in England. It is supposed to date from the victory of the Swiss army over the Burgundians at the Battle of Granson. The Swiss tried to put on their victims' coats but were unable to do so because of the tightness of the garments. They therefore slashed the material to make it looser. This impromptu style became so fashionable, and the slits in the fabric so numerous, that tailors were obliged to sear the cloth with hot irons rather than cut it with scissors. The brightly coloured lining of the garment was then pushed through the slits.

Padded jacket slashed all over and wide, slashed hat worn by mercenary soldiers in Germany

Colours

An act of Parliament of 1534 confined English dyers to the colours brown, blue, pink, tawny and violet. Materials of other colours had to be imported. A great deal of fabric was sent to Holland for dyeing and as much as £400,000 a year was spent on this trade. Cloth of gold and silver was very fashionable, though the cost of it limited its use to the very rich. Yellow was a colour worn to signify joy, and Henry VIII was insensitive enough to dress himself completely in yellow on the day that Catharine of Aragon, his first wife, died.

Jewellery

The jewellers of the English Tudor period came from Italy, France and Germany. When they settled in England they taught their art to native craftsmen. Designs for articles of jewellery were very often drawn by established artists. Holbein contributed many such designs, some of which were no doubt responsible for the fact that Henry VIII spent £10,801 on jewellery in three years. The most popular stone seems to have been the ruby, followed by the emerald and the sapphire. Pearls were everywhere. Both men and women wore elaborate brooches in their bonnets and hoods, and women wore heavy pendants on the front of their dresses. The false sleeves of the ladies were held together along the slashes by sleeve clasps, either sewn on or fastened with pins like brooches.

Children

It was usual to see children dressed in tiny versions of adult clothing. Children's clothes were made out of very fine linen or wool for the undergarments, and brocade or satin for the gowns. Tiny babies were wrapped in "body-stychets", or binding-cloths, and wore on their heads "biggins", tight linen caps which came well over the ears and were intended to help their skulls to close. Very small boys wore gowns, and did not put on hose until they were six or seven years old.

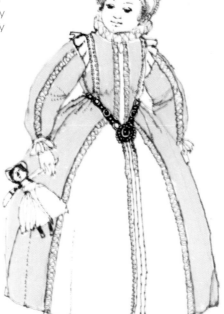

Young Tudor girl dressed in adult style costume

black felt hat

white plumes

King Henry VIII and Jane Seymour

pearl and gold brooches

gold cloth frame

jewelled gold collar

ermine collar

gable coif

cuffed, padded doublet, with embroidery

coronet, hanging down

low, square neckline

gold collar with stones

slashing

jewels

fine white shirt

leather gloves

codpiece

slashed sleeves

round-sleeved over-jacket

velvet overgown

embroidered undergown

gold lace

tight white hose

square-toed shoes

Gold brooch for hat, with precious stones and feather decoration

I bought thee kerchers to thy head which were wrought fine and gallantly. I kept thee both in booth and bed which cost my purse well-favouredly.

Greensleeves: attr. Henry VIII (1491-1547)

Man's shoe with slashing and square toe

Elizabethan

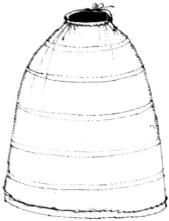

Spanish farthingale with wooden hoops

French wheel farthingale with roll cushionnet padding

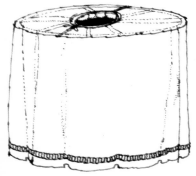

Queen Elizabeth I was very fond of finery, and when she died there were two thousand dresses in her wardrobe. The Court of Queen Elizabeth received a stream of French and Spanish visitors, and all the latest styles of those countries were copied by the English tailors and dressmakers. Literature and music reached a very high standard. The splendour of the Court was increased by the wealth brought back from overseas by swashbuckling sailors such as Drake and Raleigh.

The fashionable figure was long-waisted. Women's skirts were bell shaped in the early days, but soon developed into huge hoops. The earliest stiffened skirt, which was known as a farthingale, was the Spanish type. It consisted of a linen petticoat with steel, cane or whalebone bands inserted in it. The circular bands gradually widened from top to bottom. This farthingale was popular for many years probably because, of the various styles, it was the most convenient to wear. In about 1587 the drum farthingale was introduced from France. The hoops of this farthingale were all of the same circumference. Over the years the hoops gradually got larger until they became the vast wheels which are associated with the reign of Queen Elizabeth I.

In order to achieve the long, narrow waist, women put themselves to a great deal of discomfort. The Queen herself had a thin, flat-chested body, and the ideal was to copy this as closely as possible. Corsets were made out of leather or canvas, boned with strips of steel or wood. There is even reference to a corset made entirely out of pierced steel. They were lined with thin silk and laced up the back. The corset was put on top of the chemise. The petticoats were then put on, the top one being the hooped farthingale.

At last came the gown, which was made in two pieces, skirt and bodice. If the skirt was open up the front, an underskirt of embroidered material would be worn. The bodice came to a very deep point in the front. Sometimes an additional, triangular piece of material known as a stomacher would be attached, which reached from the neckline to the lowest point on the bodice.

The enormous skirts obviously took a good deal of managing, though girls wore them from a fairly early age and had plenty of time to practise. Not surprisingly, the hoops were very inconvenient for sitting down, and ladies took to sitting on piles of cushions on the floor.

As if the problems of the farthingale were not enough, women, and men as well, wore huge ruffs round their necks. These had begun simply as the pleated high necks of the chemise. They came into their own with the invention of starch, which many moralists looked on as the creation of the devil. One contemporary writer referred to "... starch, wherein the devil hath willed them to wash and dive their ruffs well." It could be in several colours: "white, red, blew, purple and the like."

The simplest kind of ruff was a plain band of fine linen or lawn, which was dipped in starch. It was then tied round a ruffstand while the laundress worked on the folds with a poking-stick that had been heated on charcoal. When the ruff was finished and dried it was sent back to its owner in a band box, a term

Elizabeth I wearing long-waisted gown, wired lace collar, drum shaped French farthingale

Cloak, doublet, stiff lace collar, padded short breeches, silk stockings, shoes with rosettes

Dress with padded hips, open sleeves

Ruff worn over gilt armour collar

Spanish style stuffed hat, pearl and feather decoration

which survives today. .Ruffs could be cut in points around the edges, or edged with lace or embroidery. Some people even wore two or three at the same time. The Queen of Navarre wore tiny ruffs on top of the large one in order to disguise the discoloured skin of her throat. The vast ruffs were very much at the mercy of the weather, which led to the invention of a wire frame, called a *supportasse* or *rebarto*. It was bound with silver or gold thread, or silk, and was worn round the neck under the ruff. Presumably it fastened to the bodice in front, which made the ruff stand up behind the head.

One final complication for a lady of fashion was the floor length veil. It was like a cloak of very fine gauze, wired out in two huge semi-circles at each side of the head.

The masculine outline was much narrower than in the time of Henry VIII and some men wore corsets to help them achieve this fashionable shape. Shirts were of linen or cambric. They were worn under a waistcoat which might or might not have sleeves. There were various ways of covering the legs. Round, or

trunk, hose could be any length from very short to just above the knee, and were often padded out and paned with bands of embroidered material. They could be worn with nether stocks alone, if they were quite long. If they were so short that ordinary stockings would not reach far enough, they were worn with nether stocks and a type of tight breeches called canions. The nether stocks would then be gartered over the lower edges of the canions. Canions could be of the same colour as the stocks, or could be made to match the trunk hose.

On top of the waistcoat went the doublet. It was a padded jacket which usually had a very short skirt, though this was sometimes omitted. The padded front of the doublet came down to a point below the waist, and in extreme cases even lower. Men's sleeves, unlike women's, were of reasonable size. They could be made in different material from the doublet, and were usually detachable. The ties which held them to the armholes of the doublet were concealed by a small wing, or roll of material, on the shoulder. Men wore

wrist ruffles to match their ruffs, and "a set of ruffs" would include those for the wrists as well as one for the neck.

Men had a variety of outer garments to choose from. Long or short capes, with or without sleeves, were popular as were knee length jerkins. Military, rather than civilian, men affected a short tabard known as a *mandillion*, which was open up both sides and could be put on over the head. The mandillion hung loosely from the body, and was usually stiffly lined, and decorated with heavy braid.

A love of fine clothes was no longer confined to the nobility. London apprentices in 1582 were admonished to limit their ruffs to those "a yard and a half long," before starching. Their clothing was very much on the lines of that worn by the rich, with trunk hose, canions and nether stocks, doublets (probably not padded), small ruffs and white linen cuffs. Even yeomen farmers wore everyday clothes which were similar in line to the very fashionable. They were in much more practical fabrics, however, and without excessive decoration.

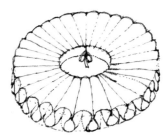

Structure of the ruff

Corset reinforced with steel strips c. 1600

Elizabethan Nobleman in traditional robes of office: white fur lined red cloak, red gown, black hat

Halberdier in uniform—red doublet with Tudor Rose and Crown, padded breeches, hose

Farmer in leather jerkin, padded breeches, hose

Hats

The flat brimmed beret, or bonnet, so popular in the time of Henry VIII, had gone out of fashion by the 1560s. Hats with high crowns were now worn by men at all levels of society. Such was the decline of the woollen bonnet that a law was passed which obliged everyone over the age of six, except those of high rank, to wear a flat bonnet on Sundays, and to be able to prove that they owned one. This was intended keep the wool trade flourishing, but the Act had to be repealed in 1597. The new tall hats could be of beaver, velvet or felt, and had narrow, stiff brims. A band of lace or braid might decorate the hat, and feathers and jewelled brooches were other adornments.

Pink slashed decoration on man's hat

Fans

Fans that were made to open and shut had been used in China for many years, but they were not introduced into England until about 1590. Even then they did not displace the old-fashioned, stiffened fabric or feather fans. An inventory of Queen Elizabeth I's possessions mentions a fan of white feathers, with a gold handle garnished with a ball of diamonds at the end (the writer noted that six of the diamonds were missing); and a fan of multi-coloured feathers, with a carefully worked gold handle and a looking glass on one side. When folding fans arrived in Europe they became extremely fashionable and men as well as women used to carry them. The carved handle and guard might be of ivory or ebony, inlaid and jewelled, and the fan itself could be made of gauze, vellum or taffeta.

Ivory handled feather fan with gold and pearl mounting

Stockings

A clergyman named William Lee invented a machine for knitting worsted stockings, but when this was brought to the notice of the Queen she paid little attention to it, as she was used to wearing hand-knitted silk stockings. Mr Lee adapted his invention to suit her, but had no success with it during his lifetime. After his death his brother, James, obtained the patronage of James I, and machine-knitted stockings became general throughout Europe.

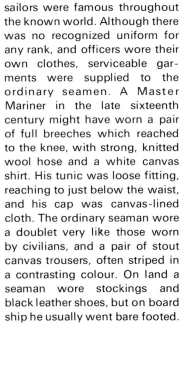
Elizabeth I in wig with pearls, and diadem headdress of gold and jewels

Outdoor gloves in brown and tan leather

Jewellery

The Elizabethans outdid even their immediate predecessors in their use of jewels. Both men and women vied with each other in decorating their clothes. A steward at Queen Elizabeth's palace noted that on April 18, 1566, the Queen wore a hat which had a band of gold enamelled with knots, set with twelve rubies, or garnets, one of which was missing. Records show that the Queen used to shed jewels at a great rate. English craftsmanship at this time reached a very high level and many beautiful pieces were produced. A favourite jewel was the tear-shaped pearl, which men wore as a single earring. It was also attached to gold and enamel brooches, pendants and necklaces.

Shoes

Most shoes were of leather that was either fine and soft or rough, depending on the price paid. Special orders were carried out in velvet, satin, silk or brocade, and could be elaborately cut and edged. Although a type of heel appeared in France at the time of Henri III, it was still unknown in England. Both men and women, however, sometimes wore cork soles on their shoes. These were higher at the back than the front, so the wearer gained extra height. The Guild of Cordwainers, or shoemakers, was granted a coat of arms by Queen Elizabeth in 1579.

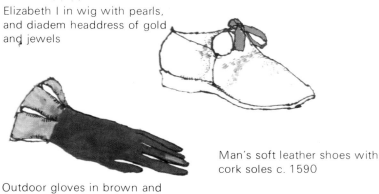
Man's soft leather shoes with cork soles c. 1590

Sailors

The English Navy was the pride of the Elizabethan era, and her sailors were famous throughout the known world. Although there was no recognized uniform for any rank, and officers wore their own clothes, serviceable garments were supplied to the ordinary seamen. A Master Mariner in the late sixteenth century might have worn a pair of full breeches which reached to the knee, with strong, knitted wool hose and a white canvas shirt. His tunic was loose fitting, reaching to just below the waist, and his cap was canvas-lined cloth. The ordinary seaman wore a doublet very like those worn by civilians, and a pair of stout canvas trousers, often striped in a contrasting colour. On land a seaman wore stockings and black leather shoes, but on board ship he usually went bare footed.

stiff, high backed collar

jewelled buttons

starched ruff

short Spanish cape

balloon sleeves

baby wrapped
in red shawl
wearing cap
embroidered dress,
ruff collar

padded peascod
belly doublet

gown with
roll farthingale

pattern in
velvet on silk

short trunk hose

white hose

soft leather shoes

Man's decorated hat

Let your attire be comely, but not costly.

John Lyly: Euphues (1579)

Embroidered leather glove
early 17thC.

Spanish Court Dress 16th and 17th Centuries

By the middle of the sixteenth century the Spanish Court led international fashion, rivalled only by the French. Spain was the most powerful of the Mediterranean countries, and had the use of enormous riches derived from the gold and silver mines of South America. The Spanish ruling family, the Habsburgs, had relatives in Austria, and Spanish styles spread through Europe. At the same time the tide of the Reformation was sweeping Europe. Philip II, who succeeded his father Charles V, was one of the most enthusiastic leaders of the counter-Reformation. His taste for formality and tradition was reflected in the extremely stiff and constricting fashions worn by his courtiers.

The Spaniards loved extravagance, yet had simple tastes in food. They were a sensual people although highly religious. These contrasting aspects brought about clothes of great luxury but comparative simplicity of line.

The earliest farthingale was Spanish, called a *verdugado*, a word derived from *verdugo*, meaning rod or hoop. Spanish women did not choose to adopt the French, drum shaped skirts. The cone shape of the verdugado was offset by enormous neck ruffs. Very tight bodices gave the effect of tiny waists and hips. As the size of the ruff grew so did the size of the skirt. King Philip IV was finally obliged to issue an edict, in 1623, against the wearing of huge ruffs. Ruffs were reduced dramatically, but skirts went on getting larger. Wide hip panniers followed the verdugado and extended the skirts even further. They, too, were limited by law, in 1639. By this time other European women had given up wearing farthingales, and the Spanish courtiers were considered laughably old-fashioned.

The sense of propriety at Court decreed high necklines. Collars were extended to such a height that the ruff acted as a headrest, giving the impression that the head had very little to do with the rest of the body. Ruffs were made of very fine lawn, trimmed with delicate lace. Women of royal birth were allowed to wear coloured ruffs.

The bodice of the dress was very tight, and corsets were even more restricting than those worn in England. There is evidence that bands of lead were used to restrain the bosom and retard its growth in order to achieve the fashionable front. The bodice might be decorated with jewels. Ropes of pearls were hung round the neck and attached to the front of the dress.

Two sets of sleeves were joined to the armholes by ties. The ties were covered by either rolls of material or by rows of silk tabs called picadils, from the Spanish word *picadilla*, meaning spear head. Picadils could also edge the bottom of the bodice.

The undersleeve was usually of material similar to the bodice. It might be braided or lightly slashed, though slashing on Spanish clothes was very restrained. The top sleeve was made out of an almost circular piece of material, folded in half and gathered into a cuff at one end. The open edges were turned back to show a contrasting lining. The underside was cut into straps, or puntas, which hung down behind the arm. The lining, which was usually of some rich material, would give the sleeve a

Piccadills covering ties of flowing false sleeve

Light vaguero with flowing false sleeves, padded shoulder epaulettes

Servant woman in gown and headdress

Lady wearing mourning mantle, leather gloves

High, flared, lace collar 1615

Cartwheel ruff 1600

certain amount of body.

The smartest way to wear this style was to allow the hand to pass through the cuff of one sleeve; and on the other, to put the hand through the top opening so that the cuff hung down behind. Another version of the hanging sleeve was also semi-circular, but had a tighter cuff and was not cut into puntas. In this case the material was heavily gold braided, and the hands were seldom worn through the cuffs. The fashion echoes the hanging sleeve of the houppelande of a hundred years previously.

Another reminder of the past was the ropa, or surcoat, which was a smarter version of those worn in the fifteenth century. It was very slightly waisted, and hung straight down from the shoulders at the back, ending well above the hem of the skirt.

Ladies at the Spanish Court remained imprisoned in their uncomfortable clothes long after more relaxed styles had been introduced elsewhere. There were times when the ladies were so tightly laced, so hugely padded and so covered in embroidery and jewels that they could move only with the greatest difficulty.

Men wore clothes which revealed and exaggerated their natural shape. The Spaniards were a martial race, frequently at war or on voyages of exploration, and civilian clothing often took on some of the shapes of armour. Tight, high-collared doublets, which came to a point in front, were worn. Ruffs, which were not as exaggerated as the ones women wore, served as a frame for the face. A fashion of about 1550 imitated the tapul, the ridge of metal which divided the two halves of the breast-plate.

Men's sleeves were of reasonable size, sometimes very lightly slashed or braided with gold. Their trunk hose varied in length from the very short to the knee length Venetian hose. The doublets and the trunk hose were padded. The very rich were able to have the panes of their hose held out with whalebone. Materials used for padding were bran, straw, and cotton waste known as bombast.

The long-waisted, pointed doublet remained in fashion until the 1590s when it was replaced by a skirted jacket with a waist roughly in the right place. This was worn with broad trunk hose which reached well down the leg to just above the knee. The sleeves were separate, and probably of a contrasting material. Spanish men are usually pictured wearing long hose, as canions were not fashionable.

In keeping with their military reputation most men wore swords and daggers. The sword belt was often passed through two or three panes of the trunk hose in front and behind.

Men had a variety of cloaks to choose from, but most courtiers wore short cloaks, which were easier to manage on horseback. Among the styles were the *capa*, a circular cloak with a hood, which could be full length or less; the *ferreruelo*, which, though similar in shape to the capa, had a high collar and no hood; the *boemio*, a semi-circular dress cloak in velvet or taffeta, sometimes lined with fur; and the *fieltro*, which was a middle-length riding cape with a collar that buttoned, and with a hood as well.

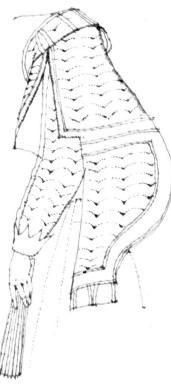
False sleeves with epaulettes covering the ties

Spanish Court costume, bell farthingale, gold embroidered dress

Peasant in rough hose, codpiece, short jacket fastened with ties, sharpening tools on belt

Nobleman in plumed hat, leather hose, doublet with fine slashing, purse on belt

Armour

Over his doublet a Spanish officer wore a highly decorated steel breastplate with a hinged steel skirt attached to it. The front of the breastplate was divided down the middle by the tapul, a sort of breastbone from which the two sides slanted away so that the armour offered no flat surface for a sword thrust. Jointed steel sleeves were attached to the breastplate, and very finely made metal gloves were worn. The neck was protected by a metal gorget, over which rose the ruff. There was a fashion for wearing civilian hats with armour, though high, pointed helmets were also worn. High ranking officers wore the sash or ribbon of their Order of Chivalry over the breastplate.

Fabrics and Colours

The Moors, who had occupied Andalusia for eight hundred years from 711 AD, had brought with them the art of weaving. Their descendants, the Moriscos, kept the weaving industry almost exclusively in their own hands. Fine merino wool cloth and very fine leather were two of the materials which were used extensively. Imported fabrics, such as silk, taffeta, velvet and brocade, were heavily embroidered with silver and gold from South American mines. The most fashionable colour was black, but other popular colours were shades of red, yellow and green. The most expensive dye was blue, and blue fabric was seldom seen, for the wealthy courtiers preferred black.

Hairstyles

It may be that the height of the ruff limited the length of men's hair. It was short at the back with two long locks on either side of the face. There seem to have been no rules about beards and moustaches. Paintings by Antonio Mor, Sanchez, Coello, Velázquez and Zurbaran show men with both or with a moustache alone or with neither. Women's hair was drawn back from the face and piled on top of the head, extending the long line of the body. Caps, feathers, jewels, pearls or little coronets might be worn on top of the hair. When the cone shaped verdugado was replaced by wide panniers, hair was dressed sideways to echo the width of the skirt.

Cosmetics

Spanish women were notorious for the amount of make-up they used. All sorts of paints were employed to make their naturally dark skins a fashionably fair colour. One writer pointed out that, when ruffs went out of fashion, the use of rouge increased enormously, as if to compensate for the loss of visual interest around the hair and face. Although a great deal of paint was used, a good complexion was admired. Elizabeth of Austria, sister-in-law of the Queen of Spain, had poultices of fresh eggs applied to her face when she had smallpox, to prevent her skin being marked.

Mantillas

The traditional Spanish mantilla began as the *manto*, or mantle, which was worn both indoors and out. The length depended on whether the wearer was married, unmarried or a widow. A widow's manto reached to the ground, and was large enough to cover her completely. When an unmarried girl went out she was supposed to wear her manto in such a way as to cover most of her face, except her eyes, as well as her dress. Fashionable women who were not so bound by the rules of decorum, and who walked in the open only when absolutely necessary, reduced the size of the manto to a formal head-covering of lace.

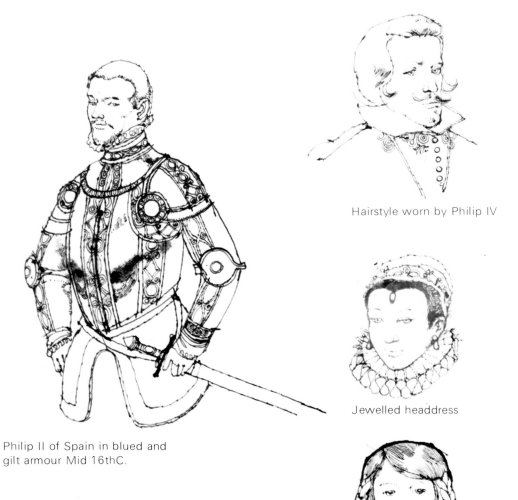

Philip II of Spain in blued and gilt armour Mid 16thC.

Hairstyle worn by Philip IV

Jewelled headdress

Plaits with red ribbon and pearl decoration 17thC.

Short mantilla with silver and orange dress laced cartwheel ruff

pyramid hairstyle

feathers, ribbons, jewelled decoration

short sleeveless gown

silk doublet

broad, soft lace collar

heavy gold chain and pendant

ed cuffs

silver lace embroidery

wide, hip panniers

handkerchief

stuffed trunk

tight hose

soft leather boots

velvet gown

Man's hat with feather decoration

Four yards of Cuenca frieze keep one warmer than four of Segovia serge.

Cervantes: Don Quixote (1605)

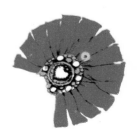

Lady's jewelled rosette for pyramid hairstyle

Dutch 17th Century

Exaggerated stomacher, gold lace, and lace ruff

Philip II of Spain inherited the seventeen provinces of the Netherlands when he came to the throne in 1555. Though there were attempts by the Dutch to throw off their Spanish rulers, it was not until 1579, when seven of the northern provinces joined the Union of Utrecht and defied Spain, that a real move towards independence was started. In 1609 a twelve year truce with Spain was signed. Finally, in 1648, Dutch independence was recognized by the Treaty of Munster. The enormous potential wealth that could be earned from the sea and from foreign trade was now for the sole use and benefit of the Netherlands. Huge sums were brought in by the fishing industry and a period of material prosperity began.

The textile industry was second in importance. Cloth was made at Leiden, where new techniques were introduced by immigrants from Flanders, refugees from the fighting there. They brought a knowledge of lighter types of cloth, and the skill for weaving them. They were so successful that by 1671 Leiden was one of the largest industrial cities in Europe. There

was a flourishing linen industry at Haarlem, where there were natural facilities for bleaching. Silk was woven in Amsterdam.

Information about the clothes worn in the seventeenth century Netherlands is particularly detailed because of the Dutch passion for paintings. Artists such as Rembrandt, Vermeer and Hals were encouraged to represent scenes from everyday life, filled with people from all classes. Paintings, which, in other countries, were usually owned only by the very rich, were bought by everyone in the Netherlands. Several contemporary writers comment on the fact. Peter Mundy wrote about paintings in butchers' and bakers' shops, and even on the premises of "blacksmiths, cobblers etc."

There were three distinct types of clothing worn in the Netherlands. One style was worn by the members of the Court, who were international in their outlook and tastes and who would follow the latest French fashion. The ordinary people appeared in another style, and the "regent" class dressed in their own particular way. The regents were the city authorities, magistrates and merchants. They were pious, conservative, staid and powerful.

In keeping with their positions of authority, the regents wore sober black clothes. To begin with these were as constricting as those worn at the Spanish Court. Their families, however, were allowed more choice. The famous painting of Burgomaster Dirck Bas and his family, by Dirck Santvoort, shows the parents wearing very formal, black, regent style clothes, while their unmarried children are dressed in the latest French style. Even the married ones have more up-to-date collars and hats. It was still thought fitting that the younger generation should wear restrained colours, and young Agatha Bas's dress, though stylish, is black with gold trimming.

A regent's wife wore a black gown, sometimes in a plain material but often, if her husband was rich and not too strict, in a velvet brocade. Her skirt would be held out by a padded, bolster farthingale, known in the Netherlands as a *fardegalijn*. She also wore a stomacher, which was much more exaggerated in shape than those worn elsewhere. In its most extreme form it jutted

Striped and ribboned sleeves, leather jerkin, long skirt

French style gown, caught up over underskirt c. 1660

Page boy in slashed suit, doublet, padded trunk hose 1634

Rubens, from a self-portrait, in jewel buckled hat and lace collar

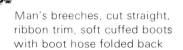
Man's breeches, cut straight, ribbon trim, soft cuffed boots with boot hose folded back

out below the waist in a sort of shelf. It was stiffened and shaped with bones and leather padding and sometimes heavily gold embroidered. The neckline of a gown was fairly low, and would be trimmed with Flemish lace. On top of the gown went the overgown, or *vlieger,* a direct descendant of the Spanish *ropa.* It began as a long, loose coat, often fastened at the neck. From about 1610 onwards it became stiffer and was allowed to fall open from top to hem. It had long, open sleeves which might have a roll of material at the shoulder.

The most characteristic feature of the dress of the regent class, and one which survived long after it had disappeared elsewhere, was the stiff ruff for both men and women. It was usually very plain but extremely wide and became known as the "millstone" ruff. The thickness of the pleats varied from about seven centimetres or less in the Northern Provinces to ten centimetres in the South, which was still under Spanish rule. Even the most puritanical women wore these ruffs. Starching them was a job for a specialist. Fashionable

people preferred a pale blue tint in the starch, but the regents and their wives wore white.

Cuffs could be of any size; from the very simple, plain white band round the wrist to deep, lace-trimmed lawn reaching nearly halfway up the arm. More elaborate cuffs might be finely pleated. Though cuffs were usually white, to match the ruffs, there are examples of black lawn cuffs trimmed with white lace.

Although they belonged to a very conservative class with strong views on modesty, the regent women followed fashion to a certain extent. When, in the middle of the seventeenth century, shorter sleeves became fashionable for women, the wives of the regents allowed an inch or two of wrist to show, but no more, for fear of being thought frivolous.

The regents' clothes were in styles that were later adopted and simplified by the Puritans of England. The regents wore black or very dark colours, but were not too straight-laced to keep up with the fashions. Various alterations to their styles took place during the years in

which they dominated the Dutch administration. Very costly materials were worn, though too much decoration was frowned on. One of the most important regents, the Grand Pensionary, Johan de Witt, murdered by a mob in 1672, was considered to have become too self-important when he ordered himself a handsome, gold-laced outfit.

The Dutch regents greatly influenced the style of clothing worn by the English Puritans. The regents, in turn, took their original, formal black fashions from the Catholic Spanish Court. We therefore have an example of strict Protestantism being influenced, albeit unconsciously, by High Catholicism.

In the early years of the century a regent wore a millstone ruff, a jerkin with a pointed and padded front, and rather baggy breeches which came to just below the knee. If the ruff was stiff enough it was held in position by the collar of the jerkin or if not, by the Dutch version of the supportasse, the *portefraes.* Regents wore black stockings and shoes. A medium length, loose coat with open sleeves was worn on top.

Young girl in cap and lace collar 1621

Young boy with millstone ruff and white cap 1621

Young man in court dress · Lady wearing silk dress with straight bodice, gold embroidery

Cavalier in breast and back plate armour, broadsword, wide top boots

55

Court Dress

The provinces of the Netherlands had formed themselves into a republic, but it was still thought desirable to have a royal leader, chosen from the House of Orange. The Prince of Orange was the head of a French speaking Court in the Hague. His courtiers all followed the latest fashions, to which they added some of their own exaggerations. Prince William II was painted wearing a short jacket over a very full shirt; full, wide breeches, or *rhingrave*, which, when spread out, could measure over six feet wide; and square-toed boots with very deep, sagging tops filled with the folds of his boot hose. He has a cloak over one arm, and the simplest part of his outfit is his plain collar, which is identical to those worn by the regents.

Hats and Caps

White linen or lawn caps were worn by most women. These started out as winged head-dresses and then took on the shape of a diadem, resting much farther on the back of the head. In order to fix the caps the head iron, or *hooftijsertgen,* was invented. It was a metal clip which went round the back of the head, with the ends resting on the cheeks. This undercap was often covered with material, and in certain parts of the Netherlands was worn on its own. Usually the fine lawn cap was pinned to it. Because the ends of the under-cap covered the ears, earrings were impractical, and a fashion evolved for attaching ornaments to the ends of the head irons. Even today it is possible to see versions of these ornaments in the head-dresses of some trad-itional Dutch costumes. A strange hat, often seen in paintings of women in churches, was a round black shape, of some hard mater-ial. It had a short stick on the top of it. From the back hung a veil of black gauze or *cyprus*, which suggests that the fashion had some religious connection.

Hair and Beards

Very conservative regent men wore their hair quite short, and had medium length, pointed beards and wide moustaches. The younger generation allowed their hair to grow longer, and trimmed their moustaches and beards, sometimes shaving the beard off completely. Regent women fastened their hair into a bun at the back of their heads, which was covered by the undercap. The more fashionable wives would allow a certain amount of fullness in the hair at the front, before it was clamped down under the head iron.

Collars

Although the regent class re-mained faithful to their millstone ruffs until the middle of the century, they were gradually re-placed by falling ruffs for the men. These were later simplified even further into plain, square linen collars, tied in front with cords. The women's ruffs became deep, starched collars which reached well over the shoulders. They might be trimmed with some very simple lace, which would match that on the plain, wide cuffs. More fashionable women wore these collars made out of heavily starched lace, in one or two layers.

Embroidery

In keeping with their slightly old-fashioned style of dressing, the regent women retained an affec-tion for heavy, gold embroidery, especially on dresses for wed-dings or other great occasions. The work was usually confined to the stomacher, or *borst*. There are many examples of such richly embroidered dress fronts, some-times with the shelf-like edge cut into flower patterns and trimmed with gold.

Accessories

There are many portraits of women carrying gloves, usually with very formal clothes. These gloves were heavily embroidered on the cuffs and trimmed with deep fringe, or ribbons and lace. Women also carried fans, usually the flat variety, with gold or painted wood handles. A regent's fashion-conscious daughter might have a black feather fan to match her sober dress.

Jewellery

A popular piece of jewellery was a heavy, gold chain. It was worn round the waist and hung down the front of the skirt. A ball of amber might decorate the end of it. A matching gold chain could be worn around the neck, and either chain or a rope of pearls could be wound round the wrist as a bracelet. Gold buttons might decorate the front of a stomacher. Wedding rings were worn, often jewelled. There was a fashion, much opposed by moralists, for wearing these on the index finger of the right hand. Earrings were not worn, as the caps which most women wore covered their ears.

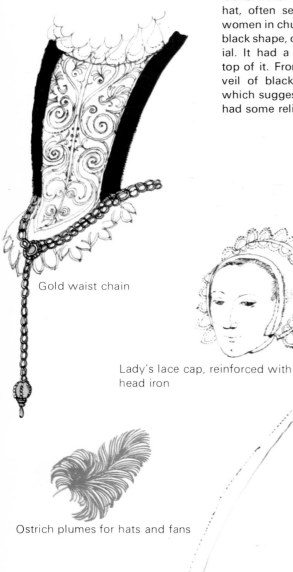

Gold waist chain

Lady's lace cap, reinforced with head iron

Ostrich plumes for hats and fans

Wide-brimmed hat, pinned up, worn over lace cap

Cap, gauze veil, tulip-like decoration of plumes and silk

Man's leather boot, turned down top, lace collar decoration
Protective leather patch

Man's embroidered leather glove

hat with ostrich plumes

orange suit of the Dutch Civil Guard

black hat with band

starched lace collar

pearl earrings

jewelled pendant in hair

hair pulled back into bun

row of buttons

millstone ruff

secondary collar

elaborate lacework decoration on stomacher and sleeves

short doublet

ornate lace cuffs

single feather fan

rapier sword

full breeches

oned garters

king stick with ribbon

underskirt

mid 17th century gown

leather shoes with rosettes

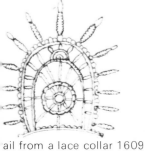

ail from a lace collar 1609

Velvet and silk are a fine recipe for putting out the fire in the kitchen.

Old Flemish proverb

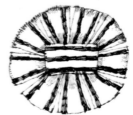

Rosette for lady's gown

King Charles I

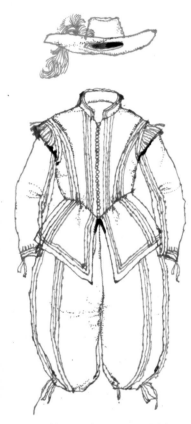

Doublet and breeches 1627

Queen Elizabeth I was succeded by James VI of Scotland. He was taken away from his French mother, Mary, Queen of Scots, at an early age and was brought up by dour Scots councillors. Perhaps because of his upbringing his Court was notably lacking in imagination. In the twenty-two years of his reign very little was introduced in the way of fashion. His Queen, Anne of Denmark, was content simply to make the clothes of the previous era even more elaborate and jewel-covered.

James's son, Charles I, altered previous fashions and gave the lead to his courtiers in matters of dress. The immediate impression given by the clothes between 1625 and 1649 is of complete change from the padded stiffness of the Elizabethan era. Starch came out of the ruffs, bombast came out of doublets and hose, men's hair grew long and women parted with their farthingales.

At the beginning of the period men wore collars which were simply unstarched ruffs. They were of two or three layers of material, measuring between seventeen and twenty-two centimetres from the high neck-band to the edge. Later on this was simplified even further into a wide collar, or band, often lace-edged and tied with cords. When armour was worn, these bands were worn outside.

The doublet lost all its padding. Though it was still very stiff and formal until about 1625, it gradually relaxed even more. After 1630 it developed into a short-waisted jacket with a fairly deep skirt. It was unbelted, and it became a widespread fashion to wear the doublet unbuttoned from about halfway down. The sleeves were usually in a "leg of mutton" shape. The complicated slashing of earlier days was replaced with one long, vertical cut in the front of the sleeve, allowing the shirt sleeve to show.

An additional garment, which might be worn over a doublet or instead of one, was the jerkin. It was a great favourite with military men, who usually had jerkins of buff leather reaching to the mid-thigh. It could be sleeveless, in which case the sleeves of the doublet would show; or, if it had sleeves of its own, the doublet was not worn. The sleeves of the jerkin, or of the doublet if one was worn, were finished with white lawn cuffs and sometimes trimmed with lace.

A new style of cuff was introduced which was to be a feature of men's coats for over a hundred years. The sleeve was cut longer than necessary, and then turned back some six inches to show a contrasting lining. It might then be trimmed with buttons, a fashion which has survived in the three or four cuff buttons which still appear on men's jacket sleeves.

The elaborate embroidery and decoration of Elizabethan dress was abandoned and trimming, if used at all, was confined mainly to the edges of jackets. Ribbon bows were used as decoration. They appeared around the waist of the doublet and were used to attach the doublet to the breeches. These bows, which had metal tips, also trimmed the legs of the breeches.

The round trunk hose of the early part of the century were now well out of fashion and only retained in some Court pages' uniforms. Breeches in the mid-seventeenth century were usually knee length, with a certain amount of fullness but no padding. In about 1630 very elegant

Cavalier, high-waisted suit, breeches 1629

Cardinal in red cloak

Altar boy in red cassock, white overshirt

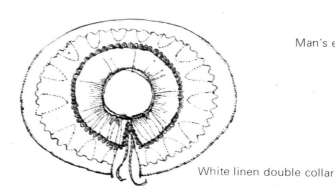

White linen double collar

Man's embroidered gauntlet

Page boy's suit, high-waisted doublet, narrow breeches, cloak 1620

men could be seen in wide, three-quarter length trousers, often trimmed with fringe.

One of the few contributions that James I made to fashion was to back William Lee's stocking knitting machine. This meant that most people could afford to wear tough, knitted cotton stockings for every day, and silk stockings for smarter occasions. These were gartered just under the breeches and, no matter how smooth they may look in portraits, they often became very wrinkled during the day.

Cloaks with wide collars were worn, either long or short as the occasion demanded. They tied round the neck with cords. An elegant man would also have had a pair of gauntlets, probably with embroidered cuffs. Some men carried short walking sticks.

Women continued to wear constricting corsets and stomachers, even though by 1630 the farthingale had gone out of style everywhere except Spain. The bosom, however, had come back into fashion in no uncertain manner and the object now was to accentuate rather than flatten it. In the early days of Charles's

reign the stomacher was part of the under dress. The gown, which might be open all the way down the front, was laced up over it. An enormous variety of collars was available, from plain linen kerchiefs, folded across the front of the dresses of Puritan women, to the elaborate lawn and lace collars that came well down over the shoulders of the fashionable.

A new style of dress appeared in about 1640 that was very relaxed in design. It consisted of a full skirt or, more often, skirts. The top skirt was cut extra long, which gave the ladies an excuse for holding it up to reveal costly petticoats underneath. Later on the top skirt was sometimes cut to open all the way up the front and was held back at the sides with ribbons or brooches. With this skirt was worn a jacket-shaped bodice with a fairly low neckline, and a hip length skirt which was usually cut into tabs. A deep lace collar or a kerchief of very fine, almost transparent lawn covered the shoulders.

For the first time in hundreds of years women showed part of their arms. Sleeves were quite

full, and probably had some sort of stiff lining to help them retain their shape, but they usually finished about half way down the forearm. They could be finished with deep, falling cuffs of lace, or pleated lawn cuffs; or even, in the early years, with little ruffles to match the unstarched neck ruff.

Women wore large, circular cloaks very like those worn by men, or long, full coats with loose sleeves. Long silk or kid gloves were worn with the shorter sleeves. Small fur or fabric muffs were carried by all who could afford them, both men and women.

The comparatively simple line of the clothes was matched by a plainness in fabrics. They were often very rich, but were usually unpatterned. A great deal of lace was used, from Venice, Valenciennes and Brussels. Rich, dark colours were popular, but so were lighter ones, which were worn by both men and women.

Children still wore miniature versions of adult clothes and must have found them a great deal more comfortable than the Elizabethan styles. Boys wore dresses until they were four.

Man's hat with plumes and ribbon

Silk dress with deep collar, gold embroidery

Boy in silk suit, short cloak

Doublet, narrow trousers, boots with boot hose, lace tops

Boots and Shoes

At the beginning of the reign of Charles I shoes had round toes. Heels, often painted red, were of a reasonable height. The sides were joined with ribbon ties, and these were covered either with silk or satin shoe roses, or left in enormous bows. Less fashionable people had their shoes fastened with leather latchets. Boots were either knee length and tight, with a wide top which fell back to reveal a contrasting lining, or calf length with even wider tops that might be lined with silk or leather and trimmed with lace. A pair of boot hose was worn over the ordinary stockings. These would be ungartered, and the loose tops of the hose fell into the wide boot tops. Boots were popular both indoors and out and spurs were often worn, whether or not the wearer intended to go riding.

Lady's white kid shoe, with gold lace trim

Jewellery

As men's hair grew longer the fashion for single earrings went out, although sailors continued to wear them for many years. Men wore rings, jewelled buttons, brooches on their hats and finely worked hilts on their swords. One of the most important items was the ribbon and badge of an order of chivalry. The most famous and coveted was the Order of the Garter. Spain had the Order of the Knights of Malta, while France had the Order of the St Esprit. The badges of these orders were originally worn on distinctive chains. In the 1600s they were worn more usually on broad ribbons across the chest. The blue ribbon of the Order of the St Esprit was the original *cordon bleu* of France. Women wore choker necklaces of pearls or semi-precious stones, and sometimes long ropes of pearls as well. The fashion for shorter sleeves allowed bracelets to be worn. They might be two or three strands of pearls wound round the wrist, or gold, jewel-set bangles. When the hair was worn quite formally dressed it could be ornamented with a pearl-decorated comb. Loosely styled hair was twined with pearls or jewelled gold ornaments.

Patches and Beauty Spots

Charles I's Queen, Henrietta Maria, was French, and brought many French ideas with her to the English Court. One of these was the fashion for beauty spots, which probably originated as a way to cover a pimple or blemish on a Court beauty's face. The best beauty spots were to be bought in a Paris shop called *La Perle des Mouches*. Names of the spots varied depending on where they were placed on the face. At the corner of the mouth they were called "kiss", perhaps not surprisingly, and "passion" if they were positioned at the outer corner of the eye. Other names were "finery", "boldness" and "coquetry". Clearly the average courtier gave a good deal of time to such pursuits. The beauty spots, or patches, were made of silk or velvet and kept in special patch boxes.

Masks

A fashionable lady protected her skin from the sun and the wind by using a mask when she went out. It sometimes covered only the top half of her face, but often a curtain of fine lace covered the lower half. These masks served a useful purpose in disguising a lady when she did not want to be recognised. Men used them for a similar purpose, particularly if they had been hired to dispose of someone's enemy or rival.

Hats

Hairstyles became softer and more informal, reflecting the mood of current fashions. Women's hair was done in a coil at the back of the head. The sides were gently curled and fell freely. A large hat would have disturbed this studied casualness, and women usually wore no more on their heads than a small white lawn cap indoors, and the hood of their cloaks outside. On horseback they wore versions of men's hats. Men wore hats of either felt or beaver, in black or brown. Brims could be the medium sized, stiff variety or the larger, soft type which were turned up at the front, side or back, according to taste. The hats might have embroidered or jewelled bands, but were more likely to be trimmed with one or more ostrich feathers in various colours.

Hair and Beards

When the stiff ruff disappeared men allowed their hair to grow to shoulder length. Some fashionable men had one side of their hair trimmed off square and the other allowed to fall in a lovelock, which usually had a ribbon bow tied to it. The small beard and moustache which is associated with Van Dyck's portraits was popular in the early years of Charles I's reign. Later these became even smaller, and many men wore a moustache without a beard.

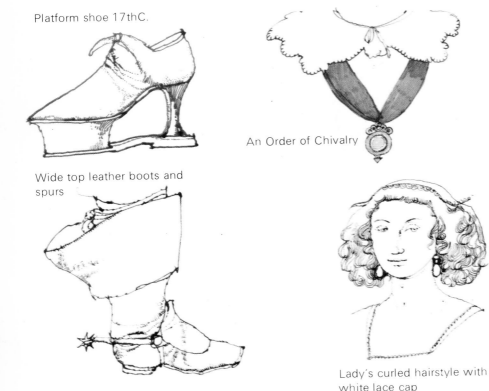

Platform shoe 17thC.

Wide top leather boots and spurs

An Order of Chivalry

Lady's curled hairstyle with white lace cap

Young man's Dutch style hat

Man's curled hairstyle, hat in the French style

black hat

white lace cap tied under chin

wide collar with lace trim

wide-brimmed hat

deep lace collar

fashionable riding outfit

high-waisted silk jacket

gold lace sword belt

gilt sword

leather riding gloves

velvet covered scabbard

knee height, soft leather boots

Middle Class Lady

spurs

King Charles I

Bodice embroidery c. 1605

Clothes do much upon the wit, as weather Does on the brain; thence comes your proverb, ''The taylor makes the man''.

Ben Jonson: The Staple of News (1626)

Brocade decoration late 17thC.

The Commonwealth 1649–1660

Charles I usually has to take all the responsibility for the events which led to the Civil War and to the following eleven years of the Commonwealth in England. The seeds had been sown earlier, however, when James I lost the trust of the merchant class by embarking on a series of foolish money-raising schemes. The clothing industry, for one, suffered a slump from which it took a generation to recover.

King James I's attention was drawn to the fact that the Dutch made at least £700,000 a year by bleaching and dyeing English cloth. They "finished it", as it was called, and then exported it. A London alderman suggested that the King forbid the export of unfinished cloth, and allow the alderman's company the monopoly of finishing and exporting English fabrics. The alderman proposed to pay the King £300,000 a year, which would have solved all James I's financial worries. The monopoly was duly granted. However, English finishing was of poor quality, and the Dutch banned its importation.

By the time King James scrapped the idea, English cloth exports had fallen by over half, and the Dutch had found new ways of obtaining unfinished cloth. Workers' wages were cut and five hundred clothiers were bankrupted. The effects were felt throughout the kingdom, as most of the spinning and weaving was still done in private homes. The clothing industry soon came to be identified with revolution.

Charled I came to the throne in 1625, and dissolved Parliament in March, 1629. Discontent was strong and the people feared that Charles, with his French wife, Henrietta Maria, was going to lead the country back to Catholicism.

The Parliamentary party in the Civil War was composed, therefore, not simply of revolutionary peasants or religious fanatics, but of men from all classes, and walks of life. The most easily recognizable type was, of course, the Puritan with his sombre clothes and a tall black hat. Not all Parliamentarians were Puritans, nor did all Royalists have long, flowing hair and clothes of silk and lace.

For the most part the Commonwealth era was a time when unnecessary ornament was banished from clothing. Very extreme Puritans did not allow embroidery anywhere on their garments, though underwear was sometimes worked with neat, Biblical quotations. Clothes were simpler, more staid versions of the Court fashions. They were less generously cut and of much more durable materials.

Parliament gave out huge contracts for equipping the army, which helped to revive the weaving industry. New techniques and materials were introduced. Worsted and serge, lighter than the old-fashioned woollen broadcloth, were made into civilian as well as military clothes.

A Puritan man wore a linen shirt and linen or cotton underdrawers. His breeches were cut fairly tight, and finished just below the knee with a very discreet ribbon tie. Although ribbons and decoration were frowned upon only the most strict Puritans tried to do without them completely. They were usually used whenever necessary. Stockings were of worsted or cotton yarn. Shoes were very sensible, square-toed and low heeled. The jacket, which reached down to the mid-thigh, was buttoned

Royalist Pikeman in cuirass (breast plate and backplate) and striped underjacket

Puritan in short coat, plain collar, hat

Puritan wife in brown woollen dress

Country wife in tucked-up skirt, short-sleeved jacket

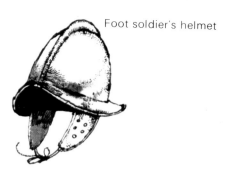
Foot soldier's helmet

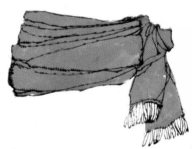
Heavy leather gauntlet and steel arm-guard

right up the front. Some of the more stylish Puritan men followed the Court fashion of leaving the lower half of the jacket unbuttoned. Plain white linen cuffs finished the wrists of the jacket. Severe linen collars were worn, tied with plain strings. Hats had high crowns and medium-sized, stiff brims. Their only decoration was a narrow band of the same material as the hat.

Most Puritans had their hair cut short, almost cropped, which earned the soldiers of the Parliamentary army the name of "Roundheads". Longer hair, if worn, was uncurled.

A garment which made its first appearance at about this time was the overcoat. It was cut very simply but used a good deal of material. Overcoats were of medium length, and had flat, square collars at the back. The sleeves usually had buttoned, turned-back cuffs.

The Puritans by no means wore black only. They used, however, less delicate colours than those worn by the Court. Brown, maroon, dark blue and dark green, violet, grey and tan were all worn by ordinary people. There was an enormous trade in

scarlet woollen material, which was used for petticoats, hoods and cloaks. None but the most narrow minded thought it irreligious to wear such a bright colour. Even Oliver Cromwell, leader of the Parliamentary troops, often wore a bright red sash with his sombre clothes.

Puritan women did not bother with such extravagances as under gowns, over gowns and stomachers. They wore several petticoats, including the bright red wool one for warmth, and probably a cotton or linen shift. Dresses were very plain, though full in the skirt. A large, linen kerchief, almost the size of a small shawl, was worn over the shoulders. It consisted of a square of material folded cornerwise and held at the throat with a plain brooch or pin. A long, white linen apron, tucked under the edge of the bodice, was worn both indoors and out. Large, hooded woollen cloaks were worn as a protection against the weather.

One curious Puritan style developed for no apparent reason. The tabs that fashionable women wore round the edge of their bodices were cut off. The one in the mid-back, however,

was left to hang like a short tail.

Most women disdained the curls of the Court ladies, and scraped their hair back into tight buns. They covered their hair with linen caps that were made in a variety of shapes. Caps were worn on their own indoors; outside, however, hats with large, stiff brims were worn on top.

The Puritan housewife wore a ribbon or chain girdle round her waist. From the end of the ribbon hung her cupboard keys and perhaps a pair of scissors. She sometimes would hang a purse, an *étui*, or needlecase, or even a kitchen knife.

By the time the Commonwealth ended and the Monarchy was restored, wealthy English people were delighted to spend their money and put an end to the sobriety of the Puritan era with a flood of colour and finery.

The Puritans who sailed to America in *The Mayflower* took with them strong religious convictions and a simple way of living and dressing. Their upbringing and the living conditions in the New World restrained them from the excesses in dress which overtook England at the Restoration.

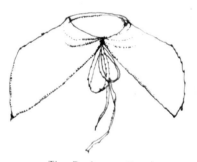
Parliamentary Army waist sash

The Puritan collar

Puritan preacher

Child in dress and cap 1658

Cavalry Trooper, Parliamentary Army, wearing cuirass, leather jerkin, sword and carbine

Soldiers

Parliamentary soldiers wore short doublets with striped sleeves underneath metal cuirasses and back-plates. They had service-able breeches, which came to just below the knee, and rough shoes and stockings. On their heads they wore basin-shaped helmets with narrow brims and small steel crests, known as *comb morions*. They were armed with cutlasses that hung from belts at their waists, and halberds. Mounted soldiers wore leather jackets over their doublets, and cuirasses on top of those. They wore long boots without the tops turned over.

Exceptions to the rule

Leading members of the Parlia-mentary faction were not as fanatical about their sober dress as some of their followers. Even Elizabeth Cromwell, the Lord Protector's daughter, had her portrait painted in 1658 wearing the smartest possible French-style clothes. Oliver Cromwell contented himself with his red sash during his lifetime, but ordinary clothes were not con-sidered good enough for him after his death. His effigy lay in state "in robes of purple velvet . . . with rich gold lace, furr'd with ermins." General Harrison, who was one of Cromwell's close Puritan associates, appeared at a reception wearing scarlet trim-med with silver lace and ribbons.

Boots

In keeping with the Puritan idea that clothes should be practical rather than decorative, men's boots were made of tough leather with square toes and low heels. Boots tops were wider than the Cavaliers' and seem to have grown in proportion to the religious fervour of the wearer. If the boots were lined it was with linen rather than silk. A pair of purely functional boot hose might be worn, but without lace or excess of material.

Jewellery

Although strict Puritans disap-proved of jewellery in all its forms, they did not manage to banish the wedding ring, though some of them preached against it as being of "heathen origin". Originally, in early marriage ser-vices, the ceremony directed that the ring should first be put on the thumb, then on the second finger, then on the third and finally on the fourth; but a curious fashion, evident in the middle of the seventeenth century, was the wearing of the ring on the thumb only. There is some doubt as to whether the ring was left per-manently on the hand, as it is now, since there are many por-traits of married women not wearing wedding rings.

Mourning

In the seventeenth century mourning could go on for a long time. Sir Ralph Verney, a gentle-man whose wife died in 1650, was still ordering new mourning clothes a year later. His list of requirements included black night clothes and night caps, a black brush and comb, black paper—though it is not clear for what purpose—and two black "sweetbaggs", which were small, spice-filled silk bags used for keeping away some of the more unpleasant smells. A widow gen-erally wore black as well, with perhaps a white set of cuffs and a white head-dress with a black "widow's peak". By the time of the Commonwealth, this peak was represented by a triangle of black material worn under a veil. Long veils of heavy black gauze were often worn for the re-mainder of a widow's life, though she would probably not wear her full mourning for more than three or four years.

Babies

It was believed that if a new-born baby was wrapped in its mother's smock it would make it attractive to the opposite sex when it grew up. Although a strict Puritan would consider such superstition immoral, the custom persisted with less religious people. An infant was dressed in a set of linen garments which consisted of six pieces: a long bib plus a separate bib collar; a strip of material which went over the head and fastened under the chin; a "stay-band", a sort of shawl with long ends which were pinned over the bib; and a broad piece of fabric which was wound round the lower half of the body.

Baby dressed in linen garments and shawl

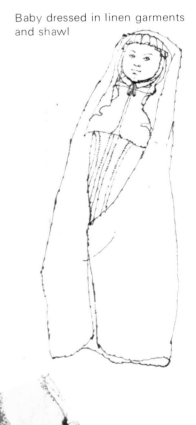

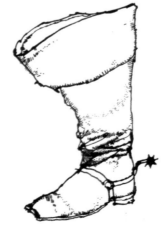

Cromwellian infantry soldier with pike and sword, wearing breastplate

Cavalry boot with broad top

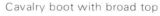

Scarlet cloak with lace collar

A widow's pea[k]
under black ve[il]

broad-brimmed Puritan hat

starched linen cap

plain Puritan collar

plain Puritan collar

arm slashes

tight-waisted grey dress

short sleeves

plain cuffs

Parliamentary
waist sash

ribbon belt with keys

gauntlet

apron

short-waisted doublet

ble-edged broadsword
basket hilt

narrow breeches

red ribbon garters

protective leather flap

spur

rough leather riding boots with
broad tops

Bow and Lace decoration
1628

Fine dressing is a foul house swept before the door.

George Herbert: Jacula Prudentum (1640)

Heavy Cavalry helmet

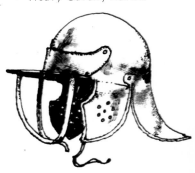

The Restoration 1660–1685

Full bottomed wig

Fashion doll

In 1660, after eleven years of Commonwealth government, the English people welcomed back Charles II as their King. Charles had spent a good deal of his exile in France, at the Court of Louis XIV, "The Sun King", and he and his courtiers had adopted many of the fashionable French ideas for clothes. The restoration of the monarchy in England was the signal for an outburst of colour and luxury in the outfits of the stylishly dressed, and lace and highly coloured ribbons were attached to whatever parts of the garments could afford space for them. The English, tired of years of Puritan austerity, were not prepared to allow any set-back to distract them, and the Plague in 1665 and the Great Fire of London in 1666 did little or nothing to halt the flood of decoration and finery sported by rich and fashion-conscious people thronging the Court and theatres.

Many of the styles popular in England were brought over from the Continent; in the first place by people who had lived there during the years of Cromwell's rule, and later by means of fashion dolls, half or one-third

life-size figures dressed in clothes complete in the last detail of up-to-date taste. This was obviously a very expensive way to learn about the latest modes; and in 1672 probably the first widely circulated fashion magazine appeared, a newspaper called *Le Mercure Galant*, which kept elegant people aware of exactly which new whim of fashion was correct to follow.

Puritan starchiness and formality gave way to studied negligence, and flowing shirts and neckwear were the order of the day for gentlemen. The poet Herrick wrote of "a sweet disorder in the dress," and the fashionable were at pains to make their appearance unstudied and casual. Every man of style wore long hair, occasionally his own, but more often a wig. To begin with, these wigs made some pretence to naturalness, but very soon they grew bigger and more artificial, though usually made in the colours of natural hair. It was rare to see powdered locks, and certainly the white of the eighteenth century was a thing of the future. Heads underneath the wigs were cropped or shaved, which led to

a fashion for nightcaps, to keep the draught off when the owner went to bed and put the wig on its stand.

Round the neck was worn the "falling band", or cravat, a wide strip of fine linen wound round and folded over in front, the ends trimmed with lace. Men's shirts were of linen or silk, and were as full and flowing as the wearer could afford. The sleeves were held at the wrist by a draw-string and richly decorated with lace that fell over the hands.

As was the case many times during the sixteenth, seventeenth and eighteenth centuries, the women were rather less elaborately dressed than the men. The materials used were often the same, and the passion for bows and embroidery, but the lines were simpler, and the decoration less indiscriminate.

A lady at Court might wear a bodice and skirt in different colours. The bodice was pointed in front and the skirt was either in one piece, or opened up the front with the sides held back by ribbons to show a rich under skirt. Bodices were laced either at the back or in front, and were cut very low indeed, though

Coat and breeches decorated with ribbons—gentleman

Merchant's wife and child in a version of adult dress

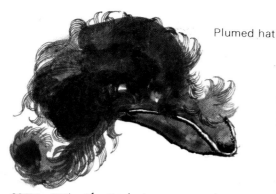

Plumed hat

Leather shoe with white heel

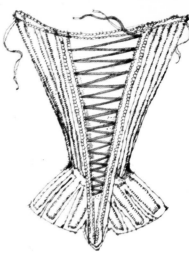

Corset with lacing and steel supports

some sort of modesty was achieved by allowing the fine linen chemise worn under the bodice to show over the top of it. Sometimes even a large lace handkerchief was worn over the shoulders and tucked into the front of the bodice. The bodice could be either sleeveless or with very tiny sleeves, which often were ribbon-trimmed. Most of the arm was covered by the chemise, which could be tied up with ribbons or pinned with jewels, according to the wealth of the wearer.

Skirts were allowed to touch the ground, except in the case of peasant women, whose skirts showed just a little of the shoes. The shoes of a fashionable woman might be in velvet, leather or silk, embroidered or jewelled; and, whereas a man's shoe sometimes had the heel and the edge of the sole dyed bright red, a woman's shoe was more likely to have a white heel, a fashion very popular in the French Court.

The women of the Restoration, though fond of jewels, wore surprisingly few of them. The beauty of the neck and the bosom was considered to need very little adornment, and a simple, single strand necklace was usually thought as much as was necessary. Sometimes women twined strings of pearls into their hair, but even these gave way to the ever-popular bunches of ribbons.

Over his shirt the fashionable man wore a very short, almost sleeveless jacket, heavily embroidered in gold or silver thread and fastened only at the neck, underneath the cravat. He wore breeches, rather like bloomers, made of dark velvet. Over those he wore a skirt which came almost to the knee and was often covered with ribbon loops, and had bunches of ribbons with metallic tips hanging from the waist. Stockings were usually silk, and either of a pale colour or white. They were secured under the bloomers, while on top of them were tight boot hose, which came up to under the knee, and were held by garters over which fell flounces of heavy lace. Shoes were black or brown. Their high heels were taken from the fashion begun by Louis XIV, who was less than five feet six inches tall. For warmth when he went out, the man of fashion could wear a cape of medium length, decorated and embroidered according to his means.

The latest fashions still took a little time to reach London, and it was not until the end of the era that a new shape arrived which was to last, in one form or another, for the next hundred years. It was a wide-brimmed hat with the brim turned up to form three points. A portrait of Peter the Great, Tsar of Russia, painted in 1676, shows this style of hat, trimmed with gold lace.

Although the King and his courtiers came back from France full of up-to-date ideas about what to wear, Charles also introduced some styles of his own. The most individual of these was the three-quarter length coat which he first wore in 1666. John Evelyn, the diarist, thought the King very smart in "a comely dress after the Persian mode." Louis XIV, who seems to have become a little impatient with his royal guest during the years of exile, made fun of Charles's "Persian" style by dressing his footmen in similar coats. The fashion persisted, however, and became the accepted top garment for the next generation.

Breeches with ribbon trimming

Country couple—simpler version fashionable clothes

Dairy maid

Ribbons and Lace

Ribbons appeared everywhere, on shoulders, on shoes, on garters, skirts, walking sticks, sleeves, anywhere that space could be found to attach a cluster. Lace was used with almost as much abandon, the lace of Venice, France and Belgium being particularly prized. It was sometimes possible to see lace combined with ribbon on men's shoes, and no man of style could be considered well-dressed without lace on his cuffs, his cravat, his boot hose and his handkerchief.

Accessories

Many accessories were used, and, as gloves were not considered particularly fashionable, being limited to the use of soldiers and horsemen, men took to carrying muffs in cold weather, often made of silk or cloth and decorated with yet more ribbon loops. They were sometimes worn on a sash or belt around the waist, or hung round the neck on a ribbon. Watches on chains were quite a usual sight. The huge wigs of the period brought about a fad for combing the hair in public and the combs were kept in little pockets in the muffs. Tall walking sticks were popular, decorated with tassels or the inevitable ribbons.

Hairstyles

Although their menfolk wore wigs, the ladies of the middle seventeenth century were content with their own hair, a good deal less formally dressed than it had been in the years before the Commonwealth. Studied negligence was as much part of a woman's dress as a man's, which may account for the restraint in the use of jewellery. It was never better displayed in a hairstyle than by Nell Gwyn, the actress who became mistress of Charles II. She had a mop of curls simply parted in the middle, giving a completely natural look. In some cases a lady's own curls could be wired, so that they stood away from her face and made a frame for it, but even then every effort was made to avoid an artificial expression.

Riding Habit

The years after the ·Restoration were the first time that women started to wear a distinctive outfit for horse-riding. Up to then they had worn their own dresses, with perhaps a hat and a pair of gloves; but now special riding dresses appeared, based on male riding clothes, and, although Pepys considered the idea shocking, the ladies took to it enthusiastically.

Materials

Much more satin was used, as opposed to velvet, and several colours were often combined in one outfit. Printed fabrics were introduced from France during the period, but they were extremely expensive to begin with, and only worn by the very rich, until the techniques of manufacture were brought over to England by the Huguenot refugees in 1685.

Embroidery

Men's clothing was often richly embroidered, a taste that the exiles had brought back from France, where the extravagant spending on costly decoration had caused Cardinal Mazarin to pass an edict in 1656 forbidding the use of gold and silver on clothes. This did not endear him to the makers of braid and embroidery, who feared that they would be put out of business, and he was forced to repeal the laws.

Colour

There was not much subtlety in the choice or use of colours in clothes—simple, bright reds, yellows, blues and greens were all fashionable, and were mixed together to an extraordinary degree on a lady's costume. The splendour in men's clothes was accompanied by a similar taste for bright colours, as if to get away from the sombre hues associated with the Commonwealth.

Suit with ribbon decoration—man's skirt and jacket

Fur muff with ribbon

Ribbon-trimmed sword and cane

Embroidered stomacher

full-bottomed wig

loose, flowing hair

short jacket
with open sleeves

silk overdress with stomacher

eeved silk shirt

falling band,
lace trimmed

wide sleeves

breeches
and skirt

lace cuffs

lace trimmed
chemise sleeves

skirt, pulled back

walking stick

hat

silk stockings

high heeled shoes with ribbons

embroidered petticoat

contrasting underskirt with
embroidery

Decorated leather shoe

A winning wave (deserving note)
In the tempestuous petticoat;
A careless shoe-string, in whose tie
I see a wild civility:
Do more bewitch me than when art
Is too precise in every part.

Robert Herrick: Delight in Disorder (c..1648)

Decorated mule

French 18th Century

Invalide of the French Army, very similar to civilian costume mid 18th C.

The heavy, elaborate styles which characterized the reign of Louis XIV of France went out of fashion after his death in 1715. They were replaced by simpler, more elegant clothes with much more attention given to the line of the body.

A move towards simplicity had been started in Rome in 1692, by an association known as "The Arcadia". The idea behind this was to replace the over-elaborate taste of the seventeenth century with a delicacy based on the imagined lives of the shepherds of Arcadia.

Clothes took on a new shape and grace. Ribbon loops were forgotten and the accent was on reason, rather than decoration. Reason was the watchword of the new age, encouraged by the spread all over Europe of a German movement towards "Enlightenment". A leading advocate of the movement was the philosopher and writer François-Marie Arouet, known as Voltaire.

In the first half of the century, France was a very prosperous nation. The merchant classes were very rich. Both men and women wore clothes of great elegance covered in embroidery and lace. The women glittered with jewels. Women had great influence, such as the Marquise de Pompadour, who was mistress of the King.

The age was represented best by the artists Watteau, Boucher and Nattier, who painted scenes of rustic charm populated by simply, but fashionably, dressed ladies and gentlemen, often sitting on swings or sharing a country picnic.

Silk and heavy muslin were used for men's shirts. They had full sleeves which were always finished with ruffles of the same material, often trimmed with lace. Down the front of the shirt were two frills of lace forming a *jabot*. The collar was completely obsolete and was replaced by a band of muslin wound round the neck and fastened at the back. Sometimes a black velvet ribbon, with a piece of jewellery pinned to the front of it, was worn over this stock. The "solitaire" was a popular, though complicated, form of wearing this black band. First it was attached to the bag which held the hair at the back of the head. Then the band was brought round to the front and fastened there with a bow

or perhaps a jewelled buckle.

Breeches were much narrower than in the previous century. They fitted snugly and ended at the knee. Sometimes stockings were gartered underneath the breeches, but it was more stylish to take the top of the stockings over the knee and fasten them there. The garters were covered by the rolled top of the stocking.

Waistcoats were longer, and fitted very closely to the body—the shape of which was improved by fairly tight corseting. Some very elaborate materials were used for waistcoats, such as brocade, satin or velvet. They could be gold embroidered or worked with tiny silk flowers, or even decorated with landscapes in *petit point* needlework. They were fastened by a great many gold, jewelled or enamelled buttons, which were left undone from about halfway down.

Coats came to just below the knee. Though they began with fairly narrow skirts, by the late seventeen twenties they had become fuller and wider. As the coat skirts grew fuller they were sometimes stiffened with whalebone to help them stand out in a circle round the body. They had

Man's suit: flared coat, wide cuffs, knee breeches, long embroidered waistcoat, ribbon tie, tricorne hat

Gown with hooped petticoat and white-embroidered underskirt, lace headdress

Watteau style, loose backed lady's dress

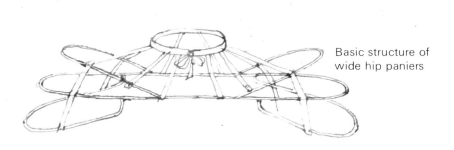

Basic structure of
wide hip paniers

Bell shaped petticoat
with whalebone hoops

Rear view of lady's
hunting jacket 1730

buttons and buttonholes all the way down the front. Sometimes a coat was left completely unbuttoned. Sometimes it was fastened at the waist and sometimes lower down or at the top. It was probably a matter of taste.

A great deal of embroidery decorated the coats down the front, on the flaps of the pockets and round the edges of the wide cuffs. The cuffs were often trimmed with buttons. It was considered fashionable to have the coat lined in material the same colour as the waistcoat. A white, lace-trimmed handkerchief might be allowed to hang from the coat pocket, for ornamental purposes only.

Black leather shoes with fairly high, red, heels were worn. They were often lined with the finest red leather, and were trimmed with square buckles on short, square tongues.

Men wore overcoats out of doors, which were cut on the same lines as ordinary coats, but had longer and fuller skirts. Alternatively they could wear long capes, which were convenient for wearing over the more elaborate cuffs and skirt of the coat beneath.

The women were as carefully corseted as the men, since a long, slim figure was considered essential. Corsets were adorned with bows and lace. Each bow was given its own name, such as *parfait contentement*, and the lace frills were called *petits bonhommes*. Skirts were made very wide by the use of paniers. These were light metal hoops which were sewn into a stiff petticoat, not unlike the farthingale but wider. The ideal was to have a great deal of width from side to side, and as little as possible from front to back. Skirts could be over a metre across but only thirty centimetres thick. Later on, the hooped skirt was replaced by two metal structures which were tied on to the hips to hold the dress on either side. Most women found this fashion inconvenient for every day, and paniers were worn only on formal occasions. They remained in fashion until the actress, Dancourt, chose to appear on stage without them.

An underskirt was put on over the paniers, then an overgown, which would have a very low neckline trimmed with a lawn or lace frill. The edges of the over-

gown's bodice could be attached to the corset, displaying the corset bows. Sometimes the bodice was laced across the front. A very popular style for the back of the dress was the sack, or Watteau, back. In this style the bodice was tight in front, but hung loosely from the neckline behind. The material fell in folds all the way to the hem.

Sleeves were usually elbow length, with wide ruffles of the same material as the dress. There were additional ruffles of lace or lawn that were trimmed with ribbon. The entire effect of great femininity was increased by the little ruff of lace or pleated ribbon which the fashionable women wore round their necks.

Skirts varied in length. A formal dress was full length, a dance dress might reach only as far as the ankle and, towards the middle of the century, even some walking dresses were shortened.

Women's shoes were delicate, made either in fine leather with red painted heels or in plain satin or brocade. The heels of brocade shoes were usually covered in the same material. They were often decorated with buckles or little jewelled brooches.

Jacket, stiff flared skirt, wig
tied with ribbon that also
ties around neck

Lady in hunting costume with
gold embroidery, worn over
hooped wide hip paniers

Peasant boy wearing sleeveless
jacket, loose shirt, wide breeches,
stockings, leather shoes

Soldiers

At about this time a recognizable uniform began to be worn by soldiers. It was possible to distinguish between the different regiments in an army, and between the different armies themselves. The uniforms were cut on civilian lines, but cuffs were smaller, waistcoats were shorter —and presumably not worn over corsets—and the coat skirts were buttoned back to allow greater freedom. Shirts and stocks were much simpler. Ruffles were not usually worn at the wrists. Officers sometimes wore steel breastplates under their coats, but for the most part these were reduced to small, crescent-shaped gorgets worn around the neck. The various regiments were identified by the different coloured facings on their coats.

Soldier's tricorne hat

Lady's tightly curled hairstyle, lace cap, satin bow

French Officer of the Guard in white uniform, faced with blue coat-flaps pinned back for mobility

Hair

The huge wigs of the previous century went out with the other fashions. Men wore their own hair tied at the back with a ribbon and with the sides curled over the ears. It might be left a natural colour, but more often it was powdered. Many men put the back hair into a black silk bag, which was held by a large black bow, while others followed the military fashion and tied their hair in a pigtail. For formal occasions white wigs were worn. As the century progressed it was considered smart to wear a wig in one's own colour and then powder it white. Women dressed their hair very simply, only adding little false curls if their own were not adequate. When they dressed up they might wear little sprays of real or artificial flowers in their hair. Madame de Pompadour took great care of her hair, and used a dressing composed of beef marrow, veal fat, nut oil and vanilla, all mixed together and scented—which must have been necessary—with oil of roses.

Man's hairstyle, with large ribbon and black cravat choker

Cavalry soldier's heavy leather boot with spurs

Materials and Colours

Silk, velvet and brocade were all used for both men's and women's clothes. Some lighter materials also came into fashion, such as bombasine, a mixture of silk and cotton. The name is derived from the Latin word *bombyx*, meaning silk or silk-worm. The fabric called grisette was a mixture of grey cotton and silk. It was used for the "good" dresses of servant girls, and in time the name came to be applied to working girls generally. A great many very pale colours were popular: blues, pinks, greens and light, creamy yellows. However, everyday clothes were often in darker shades. Men wore fine wool suits in dark green, brown or wine colour, and older women wore more sombre shades.

Page Boys

Along with the taste for simplicity went an enthusiasm for things Oriental, or vaguely exotic. Very fashionable women considered it essential to have a small, African page boy on the household staff. The boy would be the personal servant of the lady. He would be dressed as a miniature version of a fashionable man, with a befeathered, silk turban on his head. His duties would include accompanying his mistress on her shopping trips, and holding over her head a parasol, the new rage.

Young page boy in turban and red suit

Ivory handled fan with pastoral scene in watercolours

Jewellery

In keeping with the line of their clothes, women in the early eighteenth century did not wear a great deal of jewellery. There are remarkably few portraits of ladies wearing necklaces, and those show one or two simple ropes of pearls. They might consist of strands of pearls, or gold or silver work mounted with miniature portraits. Both men and women wore rings, though not in any great quantity, and both sexes carried watches. A woman wore her watch attached to a long, fine chain around her waist. A man carried his in a small pocket in his waistcoat. There was a fad among men for carrying a second, ornamental, watch in the breeches pocket, but it was the one in the waistcoat which was used to tell the time.

Accessories

Men carried snuff boxes, canes and tricorne hats. The snuff boxes ranged from very simple ones in horn or wood to fine examples of the jeweller's art, with gems and enamel work on gold, silver or tortoiseshell bases. Dress swords were worn on formal occasions. These swords were lighter than the military swords and were hung from a belt under the waistcoat in such a way that the hilt and the end of the scabbard protruded through the coat. The hilt was often in gold or silver, and might be decorated with jewels. Both men and women continued to carry muffs. They wore patches on their faces and masks when the occasion demanded. It was the time when the folding fan reached its highest level of beauty, and many famous artists used to decorate the fine silk which was stretched across ivory or delicate, enamelled wood.

tall powdered wig

white silk shirt

jabot

gold lace trim

overcoat

large gilt buttons

gold embroidery wide cuffs

full skirt

ruffled sleeves

tricorne hat

white plumes

ver buckles with ste decoration

high heels

black leather shoes

white lace ruff

corset bows down centre

elbow length sleeves

wide, ruffled lace

full length skirt

lace bow decoration

gown with lace frill edges

**Une mode en exclut une autre—
One fashion excludes another.**

Vauvenargues: Réflexions (1746)

Lady's sleeve bow with embroidery c. 1750

Harlequin figure from ribbon
718

The Fall of the French Monarchy

Neckcloth c. 1790

Hairstyle *à l'Asiatique* with oriental symbols and fruit

In the second half of the century men's clothes became slimmer while women's became more and more exaggerated. Ordinary women still wore simple clothes, but the courtiers surrounding Marie Antoinette, wife of Louis XVI, wore dresses with skirts held out by paniers. These were so wide that their escorts had to stand behind or in front of them, for they could not reach the lady's hand from the side. The Queen disliked wearing corsets but her mother, Maria Theresa of Austria, insisted that she did. She was equally firm about some of her daughter's other whims. When Marie Antoinette sent her a picture of herself in a feathered head-dress the Empress sent it back, saying that she was expecting a picture of the Queen of France but had received one of an actress instead.

The two leading creators of the new fashions were the royal dressmaker, Rose Bertin, and the hairdresser, Léonard, who was called the *Physiognomist*. Léonard designed vast hairstyles that could be anything from half a metre to a metre high, and were given all kinds of fanciful names. Together with

Mlle Bertin, Léonard contrived all kinds of hair-dos for the Queen and her Court. The ladies would try to surpass each other with bigger and better styles. The Duchesse de Lauzun arrived one day at the house of a friend wearing an entire farmyard scene on her head, topped off by a wind-mill and a pond with ducks. An advance on this, if such a thing were possible, came from an inventor called Beaulard, who designed a mechanical rose which flowered in a lady's coiffure at the touch of a spring.

Obviously these carefully created masterpieces could not be taken down and re-erected every day, and they often stayed in shape for days at a time. One writer commented that, in summer, a fortnight was the longest that "a head can go without being opened." The smell after two weeks can only be imagined, since the coiffures were usually held together by a pomade of the sort that Madame de Pompadour used to concoct.

The Queen and Rose Bertin were also responsible for making certain fabrics and colours fashionable. One day Marie Antoinette could not decide

whether or not to choose a brown taffeta for a dress designed by Bertin. The King, who saw the material, said "It's the colour of fleas." and the colour *puce,* which is now thought of as a shade of purple, became the rage. Dress designs had names such as "Stifled sighs" or "Masked desire".

Marie Antoinette disliked the formal etiquette of the French Court, and made great efforts to simplify it. In doing so, she made herself more enemies than she knew, for the old aristocrats held on to their privileges very jealously. One of the privileges enjoyed by the great ladies of the Court was to help the Queen dress in the morning. Strict rules were laid down as to who should handle which garment, and whether or not they should wear gloves while they were doing it. On one occasion the Queen stood naked while three or four courtiers wrangled over who should hand her a chemise.

In contrast to the extravagant spending on dresses by the women, the men of the time wore styles that were simpler than those of the first half of the century. Waistcoats were short-

Lady in tulle cap, looped up gown, shorter skirt, red shoes

Pink striped suit, long waistcoat, sash, dress sword

Bustle and fichu, turban-like headdress 1788

Hairstyle created during time of Marie Antoinette

A night bonnet

Young girl in stylish toque

er. Coats lost their wide, stiffened skirts and followed the line of the figure, while coat-tails made their first appearance. On grand or formal occasions the men's clothes could be just as rich as the women's, but the general effect was much more masculine than the fairy tale styles of earlier years.

Men's wigs were usually white and had a single row of curls, either on each side of the head or dressed all the way round the back. Many men still wore their own hair, powdered or in its natural colour. The very fashionable, who would not consider appearing without a wig, shaved their heads. At night time, or at home out of the public eye, a turban-like night cap was worn.

French visitors to England came back with a taste for pastoral simplicity, and from about 1780 styles changed noticeably. First to go were the paniers. Women were used to wearing a lot of material in their skirts, however, and it had to be held up somehow. A pad called a *cul de Paris* was tied at the back of of the waist, giving the effect of a small bustle. The skirt fell over this in folds of light material.

Muslin, cotton and light-weight woollen fabrics were much more suitable for the rustic effects that smart women strove to achieve.

Bodices were still tight and corsets still worn. A triangular piece of wire or metal was added to the corset in front, at the top. This was curved and padded so that from the side it balanced the *cul de Paris* and gave a "pouter pigeon" effect to the outline. Sleeves were longer and tighter, and shoulders were covered by a white lawn or cotton *fichu*.

Léonard's huge coiffures were replaced by natural looking arrangements of hair. At first these were powdered but later they were left undressed in imitation of Marie Antoinette's own soft, blond hair.

Just as the Civil War in England was the result of many and varied social pressures, so the French Revolution was as much the work of the rising middle class as of the hopelessly poor people. Many of the leading revolutionary figures were extremely fastidious, and always took care that their clothes should be clean and neat. Maximilian Robespierre wore a smart white waistcoat trimmed with

buttons engraved with guillotines. Even Marat became concerned that, because great elegance was supposed to be counter-revolutionary, it would soon be impossible to find a good tailor.

Styles were given revolutionary names, though in fact they were not all that different. The white cotton fichus which women wore over their shoulders were described as being *à la citoyenne*. The red, white and blue of the tricolour were the new fashion colours, and appeared in ribbons, rosettes, cockades in men's hats and as trim on the edges of garments. A costume for women *à la patriote* consisted of a white dress, worn under a blue coat with a red and white striped collar. Silks, velvets and brocades were not popular now, which led to serious unemployment among those who used to make them. The new cotton, wool and muslin fabrics were given suitable names, such as "Equality" and "Republic".

Young lady wearing *turban d'amour* headdress

French Revolutionary in Phrygian cap with cockade, wooden shoes, cutlass and long pike 1793

Lady in man's style long coat and hat 1789

Revolutionary official in tricolour sash 1793

Les Incroyables

Extreme fashion was thought of as typical of the unpopular royal faction. However, even during the revolutionary period there was always a group of young people ready to push prevailing styles to extremes. One such group was christened *Les Incroyables*, the unbelievables. They followed the ideas introduced by an earlier group of dandies, *les Muscadins*. They dressed in tight, high-waisted coats which sometimes had high collars, short waistcoats, and breeches which were tight to the point of indecency. Their boots were fitted to the leg, lined with contrasting materials and turned over at the top. Their amazing dress, combined with curled and scented hair, was intended as a revolt against the prevailing fashion for plainness.

An *Incroyable* wearing short waistcoat, tight breeches, tight boots, high jabot

Hats and Caps

Ordinary women wore simple lawn or cotton caps. These, however, were not enough to cover the more elaborate hairstyles invented by Léonard, and complicated arrangements of pleated and folded lawn were designed. When a lady went out she might wear a large, whalebone-stiffened hood, called a *calash*, attached to her cloak. Men who had worn tricorne hats for the first half of the century now adopted the *chapeau nivernois*. It was a shallow hat with a ten centimetre brim covered with lace, and was named after the duc de Nivernois, who is supposed to have designed it. Later, men wore beaver hats which resembled the modern top hat, though with rather more curve to the sides and the brim.

Jewellery

The most famous piece of jewellery from this period of history was Marie Antoinette's diamond necklace. Such an elaborate piece would only have been worn on State occasions. Most women, in spite of their love of display, did not usually wear much jewellery. They had jewels sewn on to their dresses, but with the introduction of the new English simplicity this fashion disappeared. Women as well as men took to wearing their watches on short ribbons or fobs. They hung from under a man's waistcoat, or from a woman's sash.

Curly hair, earrings, high jabot, large beaver hat, worn by *Les Incroyables*

Shoes

Men's fine leather shoes had reasonably high heels until the Revolution, when such extravagances were thought unnecessary. Most fashionable women, who did not set foot out of doors unless they had to, had shoes of silk, velvet and satin. Marie Antoinette had shoes with rows of emeralds set in the heels. Madame du Barry, who succeeded the Marquise de Pompadour as mistress to Louis XV, complained to her shoemaker that her shoes had worn out too quickly. He replied, "But, Madame, you must have walked on them!" When women were obliged to walk outdoors, they changed into special shoes of leather.

Turban with long feathers, and diamond and pearl earrings

High heeled, embroidered silk shoes with buckle of pearl and stone

The Phrygian cap of the Revolution

Pearl and enamel pendant c. 1790

Accessories

Snuff boxes were still extremely popular, and during the Revolution it was smart to carry a snuff box made from the lead looted from the roof of the Bastille. These boxes would often have a picture of the Bastille on the lid. Men carried canes, since dress swords were no longer fashionable. The canes were quite long and were often trimmed with bows or tassels. Even women carried tall canes when they went out walking. Umbrellas and sunshades were made of fine leather, oiled cloth or painted paper. They could also be made in silk or taffeta to match a dress. A very successful introduction was the *eau de Cologne*, made by the brothers Farina, two Italians who had settled in Germany.

Children

Young children, who had been forced to wear tiny versions of adult clothing for so long, finally were released into something more suitable for their age. The style came from England, where it was fashionable to dress boys like "English sailors", in trousers, little waistcoats and short jackets, so that they would have more freedom to move. French boys started to enjoy this freedom in about 1778. The little girls were fortunate as well, having been bound up in laces and whalebone until the middle of the century. They now had dresses in muslin and printed cotton, with ankle length skirts and high sashes.

Child in comfortable su and cotton cap

tall black hat

patriotic suit
with red facing
in military style

tall beaver hat

ur cockade

curled hair

black cravat

natural curly hair

short waisted,
double breasted coat

lace jabot

shirt with red trim

long, square-cut
waistcoat

tight, white waistcoat

red cuffs

ruffled shirt cuff

ruffled shirt
cuffs

gold watch
chain

red military style
decorations

tight black
breeches

stockings

walking cane
with gold top

black leather shoes

shoes with buckles of
metal and paste

It is better to leave the Mode to its own vagaries.

Horace Walpole (1781)

Lady's feather-decorated
bonnet 1792

Lady's bonnet with bows
1793

Late Georgian, English and American

Ribbon bow for fastening lace cap at back of the head

Young girl in caraco jacket and cap decorated in the French style

The English taste for simplicity, which influenced French fashion in about 1780, stemmed from the life style of the prosperous middle classes. It was based not so much on the smart life of London but on the styles most suitable for their farms and for country houses.

The Adam brothers designed and decorated houses in the classical style and often designed the furniture as well. The entire effect was uniformly delightful to the eye. The great English cabinet makers, Hepplewhite, Sheraton and Chippendale created furniture with clean lines, beauty and strength. The simplicity of the architecture and the beauty of well-made furniture were echoed in the well-cut, unostentatious clothes which were the hallmark of the English gentleman. Lord Chesterfield, who wrote a series of letters to his son, reminded him that the best suit of clothes was one that did not call attention to itself.

Men's shirts were usually made of a kind of fine linen called cambric. They had small ruffles down the front and at the wrists. A stock of the same material was wound round the neck. To-wards the end of the eighteenth century it was possible to see the beginning of a new style, with the points of a collar showing over the top of the stock. In this case the stock might be tied in front in a small bow.

Breeches were still tight, but by now were long enough to reach over the knee, with silk stockings gartered underneath them. Embroidered patterns, clocks, were often seen decorating the ankles of the stockings. It was thought most important to have one's breeches fitting well, as the shorter waistcoats and cutaway coats showed off every wrinkle. The doeskin breeches worn for riding were particularly smooth and tight.

The long waistcoat of the early part of the century was now replaced by a shorter garment. It was often double-breasted, with lapels which were allowed to show outside those of the coat. Coats had high, turn-over collars. They were made to button right up to the neck, though they were more usually worn open all the way down. Although cuffs on coat sleeves had more or less gone out of style by 1780, two or three buttons with button-holes were left as decoration on the sleeve.

Men's shoes were plainer and had lower heels, which by now were usually the same colour as the shoe, rather than red. Shoes were often decorated with discreet silver buckles. Boots were worn outdoors and for riding. They were usually black, with a contrasting tan lining showing over the top.

Men still wore cloaks, but the calf length overcoat had become more popular. It had two or three capes at the shoulder, a style which is always associated with highwaymen. These "gentlemen of the road" were very fashion-conscious, in fact. If they were caught they went to great trouble to dress up for their execution, which would be attended by crowds of people ready for a day's entertainment.

American styles were very similar to those worn in England, as shown by John Trumbull's painting of the men who signed the Declaration of Independence. European fashions took some time to cross the Atlantic, and Americans never went through the same elaborately brocaded and powdered phase that the

American naval commander in dark blue uniform with red facing, long-waisted red waistcoat, gold trimming 1786

English gentleman in light grey frock coat and breeches 1780

Preacher wearing black

Lady's butterfly cap of lace and ribbon 1776

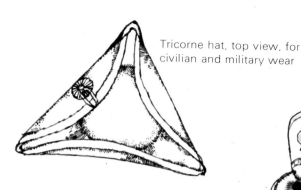

Tricorne hat, top view, for civilian and military wear

Leather helmet with badge of St George, red horsehair plume, brass fittings 1776

French did. For the most part they were too busy building their nation. Their liking for informality was apparent. John Singleton Copley's portrait of Paul Revere shows him in his shirtsleeves, with no cravat, and with waistcoat unbuttoned.

George Washington's Army was not uniformly dressed during the War of Independence. However, the General required his men "to shave, have clean hands and a general air of neatness." Washington complained that his soldiers were "not, like the Enemy, brilliantly and uniformly attired." The British Army was dressed in scarlet coats. They wore curiously pointed hats, and gaiters which reached half-way up their thighs.

A slightly masculine look in dress was adopted at this time by some English women. It showed particularly in the *redingote*, which was a travelling costume consisting of a long skirt, a shirt with a cravat and a tight waistcoat. A full length coat with two or more capes on the shoulders was worn on top. All kinds of hats were permissible with this very tailored outfit, from the straw

"shepherdess" style to the big-brimmed, velvet or beaver hats.

Women's clothes generally became softer and muslin and silk gauze were the most popular materials. Muslin could be sprigged, embroidered with coloured silks, or gold or silver threads. It was used for formal as well as informal dresses.

Towards the end of the century there was a vogue for Grecian styles. As far back as 1755 people of fashion had been impressed by the discovery of the remains of Pompeii, but the Roman clothes were obviously unsuitable for modern wear. Greek styles, however, were much simpler. Women began to abandon their corsets and shifts, and started to wear very simple dresses, belted high under the bosom. No undergarment other than a plain, flesh-coloured, knitted silk vest was thought necessary.

Muslin was the most suitable material for these new dresses, and many different kinds were advertised. Moravian muslin, which is now known as *broderie anglaise*, was cut with very small holes which were then embroidered round the edge in the

same colour. This was an expensive fabric, but other versions of the same material were cheaper. Because the slimness of the dresses prevented the wearing of heavy underwear, velvet jackets and over gowns in contrasting colours were worn in cold weather.

A peculiarly English style, which caused a good deal of comment when it was worn on the Continent, was the riding habit for women. This was always made by a man's tailor. It consisted of a jacket and waistcoat cut like a man's, and a long skirt with a small train. The habit was always made in good woollen cloth, though the waistcoat was often made in silk or satin, in a contrasting colour to the rest of the outfit. While very pale colours were essential for the light muslin frocks of the day, darker colours were used for riding clothes. At one time these habits were worn on other occasions. In 1782, women were seen wearing riding habits at a ball. They went out of fashion for a very short time, but by 1790 they were popular again, as riding was an integral part of the pastoral life of any English country gentle-woman.

Girl wearing gown looped up, blue shawl, tulle cap 1785

English grenadier officer from the American War of Independence wearing bearskin cap, high stocks, brass gorget

far left:
English cavalry officer in red coat, yellow facing, black stock, maroon waist sash, white buckskin breeches; brass gorget, showing rank, around his neck 1785

Young girl in gown of lawn, long coloured sashes, hat with ribbons and feathers c. 1790

Materials

A great many of the materials used at this time were imported from India and the Far East, as the British East India Company controlled a large amount of the commerce from those parts. Cotton materials were imported from India, and silken fabrics from the Orient. There was a flourishing textile industry in England, producing woollen fabrics such as broadcloth, kerseymere and the strangely named fearnought or dreadnought, which was a thick cloth with a long pile used for outer garments. Most of the lighter fabrics were in pale colours, but the woollens were in bottle green, brown, burgundy and snuff-colour. Bright scarlet had not yet gone out of fashion.

Bathing Dresses

Sea bathing was declared a remedy for all sorts of complaints, and resorts such as Brighton, Blackpool and Dover were visited by ladies and gentlemen wishing to take a cure. It was a very serious business. On the morning that she intended to bathe, a lady would put on a long, flannel gown under her ordinary clothes and proceed to the beach. There she would take off her top clothes and hand them to an attendant. She would then venture into the sea and submerge herself completely, as many as twenty times. Ladies wore flannel bathing caps over their hair but, as the cure was most successful if total submersion took place, the caps cannot have been of much use.

Accessories

While full skirts were fashionable, women used to wear pouches, or pockets, hung round their waist under the skirts, which could be reached through slits in the top material. With the introduction of the new, slim dresses, these pockets became impractical, and women started to carry handbags. To begin with they used their work bags, or knotting-bags, in which they put their gloves, their fans and little bottles of smelling salts or eau de Cologne. These knotting-bags were gradually replaced by soft bags that were held at the top with a drawstring and known as reticules, or indispensables. Men and women both carried long canes and umbrellas. Women used to wear flowers, which were kept fresh in small bottles of water that were attached to their dresses. Watches, which had been extremely fashionable for some years, went out of style for women when the thin, light dresses were introduced. Men still wore them as fobs, hanging on short ribbons below their waistcoats.

Boots and Shoes

Women's shoes at this time were made of satin, brocade or kid, and had reasonably low heels. A "Chinese" slipper, which had a turned-up toe, was introduced in the middle 1780s. A version of this, fur lined for winter, was known as a *Kampskatcha* slipper. For riding or walking, women wore boots of soft leather, which reached to just below the knee. They could wear wooden pattens to protect their shoes on muddy streets.

Lady's embroidered shoes 18th C.

Lady in flannel bathing gown and bathing cap

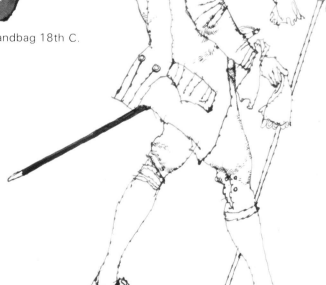

Lady's satin handbag 18th C.

A Macaroni dressed in tight-fitting clothes and wearing high wig 18th C.

The Macaronis

The simplicity of the age produced a fashion group in England comparable to *Les Incroyables*. They were known as "Macaronis", so called because they affected foreign styles, particularly Italian ones. Every item of their clothing was extreme, from the very high wigs with tiny hats perched on top of them, to the little shoes, often decorated with ribbon rosettes. One affectation was to wear enormous buttons on the coat. The Macaronis were carefully corseted, and their breeches, waistcoats and coats were expected to fit as tightly as possible. The fashion was seen occasionally in America, where "Yankee Doodle went to Town," when he put a feather in his cap "and called it macaroni."

The Purple Heart

The principal American award for gallantry was introduced by George Washington in 1782. Enlisted men who displayed "unusual gallantry and extraordinary fidelity" were allowed to display a heart-shaped piece of purple cloth on the left breast of their uniforms. At the time it does not appear to have been a very frequent award, and after three or four presentations it fell into disuse, but it was revived in 1932 as a presentation to those wounded in battle.

The Purple Heart patch of the American Army

Lady in Macaroni hairstyle

Lady of latter half 18th century

white lace cap

ribbons and feathers

green silk fan

frill collar

pearl necklace

ivory handle

white lace frills
down front

half length sleeves

frill trim

gold bracelet

French style
satin gown

white frill trimmed underskirt

Fashionable country squire
in riding outfit

black tricorne hat

rosette decoration

powdered wig

loose frilly shirt

dandy hairdo
of long plaits

lace front on shirt

brass coat buttons

tight yellow
waistcoat

large
handkerchief

red hunting coat

buckskin
breeches

tops
turned down

black and tan
riding boots

spurs

Bird motif on ribbon

**Dress doth make a difference, David.
'Tis all in all, I think.**

Sheridan: The Rivals (1775)

Flower decoration on
silk brocade

The Directory and the First Empir

Merveilleuse lady in wide skirts with flounces, huge ribbons on head

The effects of the French Revolution were disastrous, not only for the aristocrats, who had lost their homes, possessions and families, but also for poorer people. The country lacked leadership and was badly managed during the period of the Directory, 1795 to 1799. Very few foreign countries supported the revolutionary regime and the export trade almost disappeared. The linen and textile mills of Brittany and the Languedoc stopped operating, and no lace was made in Valenciennes. Business in some towns was so bad that many of the tradesmen no longer found it worth while to open their shops.

As often happens in times of trouble there were people who hid their heads in the sand, and attempted to look as elegant and useless as possible. *Les Incroyables,* with their exaggerated clothes and curled hair, were partnered by women known as *Les Merveilleuses.* They carried the classical Greek idea of clothing to extremes.

Their sole undergarment was a pair of pink, silk body tights. Over these they wore muslin dresses so skimpy as to be barely decent. They even went so far as to dampen the dresses, in order to make them cling more closely to the body. The neckline was always extremely low but the smart *Merveilleuse* might wear a muslin neck-cloth, like a man's, tied round her throat. She carried a long gauze or silk stole. The most fashionable hat fitted tightly to the head and resembled a jockey's cap, with an enormous, beak-like front brim. Tiny flat sandals were worn, sometimes with ribbons that were crossed over and tied up the leg in imitation of the classical style.

Napoleon Bonaparte was created First Consul in 1799, and Emperor in 1804. One of his first tasks was to restore the economy. In a fashion-conscious country such as France this depended a good deal on rebuilding the textile industry, for a lot of ground had been lost during the Revolution. Spinning and weaving were still done by hand, whereas in England Arkwright and Watt had invented machines for the jobs. Napoleon banned the importation of English textiles. He started factories at Sedan and Louviers, and revived the lace industry of Valenciennes. Other

fabrics were made there such as tulle and batiste, a material similar to cambric, named after its originator, Baptiste of Cambrai.

Napoleon also tried subtle ways of persuading women to wear more clothes. He began by piling logs on to the fires at some of his receptions, sympathizing with his female guests because they must have been so cold. When this did not work he had the fireplaces at the Tuileries bricked up, so that women had to dress more warmly. He also forbade ladies to appear at his Court wearing the same dress more than once.

The most influential man in the sphere of fashion was the dressmaker, Leroy. Just before the Revolution he had been hairdresser to Marie Antoinette, but somehow he had managed to survive the Terror. He became dressmaker to the Empress Josephine and, through her, to practically the whole Court. He employed a large staff, all of whom were well paid and supplied with board and lodging. He was in Napoleon's confidence and helped the Emperor in his efforts to re-establish the textile mills, by designing clothes which used a

Boot shine boy in ex soldier's cap, neck scarf, baggy trousers, short jacket

Large neck cloth, boots with tops turned down, untidy powdered hair c. 1807

Flimsy chemise dress of transparent muslin c. 1807

Large-brimmed straw hat

Incroyable fashion of high neckcloth, untidy hair, and patriotic hat

Busby of the Chasseurs of the Imperial Guard 1805

great deal of expensive material.

Leroy's effect on the classical styles has been known ever since as the *Empire* line. This is exemplified by a graceful, uncorseted figure in a flowing gown of soft material belted high under the bosom. The style expressed a sense of decorum which was completely absent from the gowns of the Directory. The Empire style was first seen at the Coronation of Napoleon and Josephine, when the Empress and her ladies wore dresses which had been designed, in fact, by the Court painter Jean-Baptiste Isabey but made by Leroy in his workshops.

The basic Empire line dress had a very low neckline. Sleeves varied. For the evening a tiny puffed sleeve that hardly covered the shoulder was considered enough. Day dresses, however. might have sleeves to the elbow, or even covering the hand, in a style called *à la mamelouk*. Cashmere, velvet and crêpe were popular for day dresses. Out of doors they were usually worn with long, high-waisted coats. Evening dresses were of sequinned tulle, satin and taffeta.

It was a time of great en-thusiasm for furs. Capes and tippets were made from lynx, astrakhan, ermine, blue or silver fox and, rarest of all, chinchilla. These last were enormously expensive, and only four or five of the richest women in Paris owned one.

Napoleon did not spare the men in his drive to restore the prosperity of the mills. On formal occasions generals, marshals and politicians were obliged to appear wearing white satin breeches and brightly-coloured silk coats, heavy with embroidery.

During the day much more practical clothing was the rule. The shape of the coat had changed considerably: it now had long tails, cut off square just behind the knee, and a square-cut front, with a couple of inches of waistcoat showing beneath it. Collars were quite high, and formed revers on the front of the coat. Sleeves were often gathered at the top into a slight fullness. The ruffles on shirt cuffs were seen less frequently. Shirt sleeves were usually finished with a plain band and two buttons, which were often left unfastened. Lace was worn at the wrists with the silken Court clothes, but other-

wise had gone completely out of fashion.

Breeches were still worn, particularly with formal dress, but a new leg-covering had been introduced, the pantaloon. When worn with boots these could easily be mistaken for breeches, as they were just as close fitting. They reached to half-way down the calf, however, as opposed to just below the knee. They were fastened with three plain buttons. The tight style of pantaloons was made from a knitted elastic wool fabric. Early in the nineteenth century the style became slightly looser and ankle length. These pantaloons were cut from kerseymere, a fine cloth, woven with a diagonal ribbing that allowed it to give a little.

The longer pantaloons, or "trowsers", often had straps which passed under the feet. Summer trowsers might be made of nankeen, a heavy Indian cotton cloth of a yellowish brown colour, or of heavy cotton *jane* or *jean*. Indoors, with either their breeches or their pantaloons, men wore black slippers, though light boots were not thought out of place. Leather boots were the usual wear for out of doors.

Broad-brimmed outdoor bonnet, loose gown

Lady in chemise gown with long train, falling from sleeveless waistcoat 1801

An *Incroyable* with beaver hat, wearing long coat with broad striped lapels, tight yellow breeches 1801

Napoleon in uniform with long tail-coat white waistcoat, gold epaulettes, red facing

Napoleonic military drum

Hats

As long ago as the early nineteenth century there was an Easter Parade, which in Paris was called the *Promenade de Longchamp*. Ladies of fashion took this opportunity to show off their new dresses, carriages and, particularly, hats. These were all sizes, from tiny caps to enormous, ribbon-covered bonnets. When Madame Récamier, one of the smartest French women, visited England in 1802 she contented herself with throwing a large veil over her head when she went out. This, "not unnaturally, caused her to be followed and stared at." Other ladies wore turbans, military looking top hats with peaks, or jockey-like satin bonnets trimmed with ribbons and feathers. Imitation flowers were a favourite form of trimming, and an enormous spray of arum lilies could be used to adorn a tall straw hat with a wide brim.

Hair

Women's hair styles appeared to be fairly simple and were designed to harmonize with the classical lines of the Empire dresses. In fact, quite a lot of false hair was used to produce ringlets, chignons and falls. If a contemporary advertisement is to be believed, the hair was taken from French peasants, and then treated by washing and baking to produce natural looking curls. Men had their hair cut fairly short, except a few old-fashioned souls. If it was not naturally curly the men had their hair curled and brushed into a loose, casual style, with side-whiskers reaching half-way down the cheeks.

Jewellery

By this time men had more or less completely given up wearing jewellery, perhaps with the exception of a simple gold ring or a small diamond pin in the shirt front. For formal occasions they might wear an order, either hung round the neck on a short ribbon or pinned on the jacket. Women wore jewelled combs in their hair, or pearls, or tiaras which were modelled on Greek styles. Simple necklaces and bracelets were also designed from Greek originals, and with shorter hair fashionable once more earrings regained their popularity. Jewellers started to make matching sets, which included a necklace, a tiara, a pair of earrings, bracelets and a brooch.

The diamond and pearl necklace of the Empress Josephine

Hairstyle of ringlets and chignon

Back view of lady's curled hair and elaborate collar

Outer Garments

While men continued to wear their caped top coats, usually made out of broadcloth or other woollen materials, women had a much larger variety of outer garments to choose from. One of the most popular was the shawl. It was usually square and folded corner to corner to give a triangular shape. The spencer was a small coat of English origin which was worn indoors and out. It was like a little waistcoat and was worn much in the same way as a cardigan is today. It might have no sleeves at all or long, tight ones. It could be buttoned up to the throat or left open. Pelisses were long coats worn outdoors over dresses of a lighter colour. Pelerines were little shoulder capes, usually of velvet, trimmed with fur.

Motifs and Decoration

In the years of the Directory and the beginning of the First Empire decoration of fabrics and clothes was inspired, like so many other things, by classical Greek originals. Geometric shapes were worked into borders which trimmed the edges of dresses and hats. At the turn of the century some slightly Eastern patterns were introduced, as a result of the exotic presents brought back from Napoleon's Egyptian campaign. Decoration and embroidery were very delicate when the classical styles were most closely followed, but became coarsened, as did some items of clothing, when prosperity returned to France during the Empire.

Accessories

Gloves came back into fashion for men, and were made out of fine kid, often dyed to match the colour of a suit. Riding gloves, which were of a tougher material, were brown or black. Women's gloves were short for day wear, and very long with evening dresses, reaching almost to the tiny sleeves. A lady's gloves usually matched her dress, though white was the most popular colour for the evening. Men carried canes or swordsticks; women had parasols, fans, muffs and reticules. Madame Tallien, the wife of one of the Revolutionary leaders, was one of the first women to carry a reticule. She owned several made from soft fabrics, and others that were made of papier mâché or enamelled tin, shaped like a Grecian urn.

Informal cotton bonnet

Bonnet with floral decoration

Jockey style bonnet with ribbons

Poke bonnet with beak-like peak in front

Man in green spencer jacket over black tail-coat 1808

French couple 1810

tall beaver hat

yellow silk bonnet

high collar

ribbon fastenings

cravat

white waistcoat with red trim

blue outdoor pelisse

short Vandyked sleeves

sleeves *à la mamelouk*

soft leather gloves

walking cane

set-in, paisley patterned panel

long, tight-fitting pantaloons

white stockings

matching buttons

soft shoes

Jockey type satin bonnet c. 1809

Fashion constantly begins and ends in the two things it abhors most— singularity and vulgarity.

William Hazlitt (1778-1830)

Decorative motif based on the initial of the Empress Josephine

The Romantic Period 1815–1840

British Army officer c. 1835

Morning dress in brown silk, bishop sleeves c. 1837

At the end of the eighteenth century and the beginning of the nineteenth men's clothing stopped trying to compete with women's in splendour and style, and settled down very much on the lines that we know today. It was a time of great mechanical and industrial progress. Gas lighting was installed in public buildings in England and France, steam trains reached the unheard of speed of thirty miles an hour in 1830, and a steam ship crossed from Bristol to New York in fifteen days. The pace of life quickened to such an extent that men began to think in terms of more practical, comfortable clothing for every day and reserved their finery for the evening. Full evening dress today has changed very little from what it was in 1830.

The change in men's clothing did not happen overnight, and to begin with the male outline looked much as it had done in the days of the Empire. The waist of the tail coat was now roughly where it ought to be, and was not cut high. The slight fullness at the top of the coat sleeve increased. A full-skirted frock coat was introduced for riding. This

garment became the typical Victorian daytime wear for men, and lasted well into the twentieth century. It has not completely disappeared and is still seen at very formal weddings.

It was the famous dandy, George Bryan Brummell, known as "Beau" Brummell, who introduced the starched collar. He created quite a scandal by wearing something other than the fashionable neck-wear worn by the Prince Regent. Once Brummell had worn a starched collar, however, everyone else took up the fashion. Very elegant young men used to wear their collars so high that they cut their ears if they moved their heads too quickly. The cravat or necktie, arranged in one of several ways, was worn outside the collar. An Italian set up a school for cravat tying in Paris, at fifty-four francs for each six-hour lesson. Elaborate illustrated instructions were issued in books, showing twenty or more different styles of cravat including *Orientale* and *à la Byron*. Collars were attached to shirts by studs or buttons.

Breeches were still obligatory at Court, and were often worn for riding, when they were known

as "smallclothes" or "smalls" Trousers, however, were now worn almost everywhere. They were very full at the hips, narrowing to the ankles where they were held under the foot by a strap.

In the eighteen-twenties and thirties it was smart for a man to have a small-waisted, feminine figure. This was often achieved by the use of corsets, which were put on over the shirt and trousers and then laced to the required size. If a man thought corsets too restricting he could wear a waistcoat with lacing up the back.

These waistcoats were the sole survivors of the colourful clothes of the previous century. They were the only garments where men allowed themselves a little variation from the sober colours that were used for their top clothes. Waistcoats were made out of striped or embroidered silk, velvet or satin, and might have gold or jewelled buttons. They were so fashionable that the French poet, Alfred de Musset, ordered thirty-one different waistcoats all at once.

Once corseted, cravatted, trousered and waistcoated, a man could put on the coat appropriate to his activity. A tail coat, very

Party dress for young girl, elaborate turban headdress 1831

Morning dress for men, top hat light colour trousers, dark

jacket, striped waistcoat, cravat, walking stick 1834

A la Byron

Irlandaise

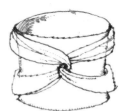

Orientale

Lady's chemisette with frills c. 1828

like those of the early part of the century, was worn ordinarily. The longer-skirted frock coat was worn for riding or shooting. By 1830 the frock coat had put the tail coat completely out of fashion, and was worn every day. It was usually single-breasted, and had a large collar that extended over the shoulders.

Outdoors, men wore heavy overcoats cut on the same lines as the frock coats or cloaks with fur collars. In 1836 some men started to wear waterproof topcoats in "Mackintosh's India-rubber cloth". Far from being useful, these garments were sneered at by the writers in men's fashion magazines, who commented that: "No one can look like a gentleman in such a garb," and pointed out that the smell was enough to put most people off. In fact, these waterproof coats became rather a nuisance in the cities. The smell was so strong that they were unpopular on public transport.

The top hat was almost universal head-gear for men. It had come a long way from that day in the late eighteenth century when an English hatter who appeared in a high silk hat had been

charged with breaching the peace. The sight had caused a riot, during which women fainted and a small boy had his arm broken. By the middle of the nineteenth century all these alarms had been forgotten and the shiny black silk stovepipe was a favourite for townsmen.

The sobriety which now characterized men's clothes did not extend to women's dress. The classic Greek lines, so popular during the Directory, became decorated with ribbons and flounces. Restoration of the French monarchy in 1814, combined with the new prosperity of the French textile industry, led to the return of tightly corseted waists, huge sleeves and wide skirts.

Styles in the eighteen-twenties were very attractive. Dresses had high necklines, often with a little collar. Sleeves had filled out into the gigot, or leg o' mutton, shape and reached to the wrist. The skirt was bell shaped and was often trimmed with ribbon or braid. A number of petticoats were worn underneath to give it fullness. The fashionable length for a skirt was just at the ankle. The

tiny waists were emphasized by belts of the same material as the dresses.

Later in the period necklines became lower, though they might be filled in with pleated lawn tops gathered into a little ruffle at the neck. Sleeves became larger. The leg o' mutton sleeve was made even wider. A larger variation was known as *à la folle,* in the style of the madwoman, a name which might have been deserved.

Skirts were fuller, and padded out at the back with either a crescent shaped bolster or a series of stiff frills sewn on to a piece of material, which was tied round the waist under the petticoat. This was the bustle, or false bottom, which was worn by all classes. Carlyle's wife noted that "the very servant girls wear bustles," and went on to tell of one maid who pinned three dusters under her dress as a bustle. Sometimes these make-shift arrangements were not successful, and the writers in fashion magazines were critical of bustles which made the back of a dress look lumpy, as if "some domestic utensil were fastened under the dress."

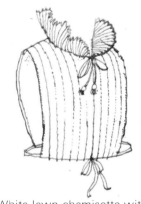

White lawn chemisette with pleated frills around neck c. 1820

Young lady in outdoor dress, gigot sleeves, feathered bonnet, transparent veils, parasol, handbag, 1834

French farm girl in striped shawl, heavy brown dress

Riding habit in a masculine style 1840

Children's Clothing

Children's clothes were comfortable and practical early in this period, though the fashion of putting little boys into dresses still persisted. From the age of about five or six, boys would wear long trousers, or "pantalettes". A knee length tunic was worn on top, often with the wide shirt collar showing at the neck. Older boys wore long trousers and short jackets. Boys were allowed to wear longer hair than adults, and they wore either peaked, soft caps or floppy velvet berets. Girls, from about 1825 onwards, were once again forced into garments as much like their mothers' as possible. They wore pantalettes often lace-trimmed, which reached to their ankles, and wide, ribbon-covered skirts.

Women's Outer Garments

Women, as usual, had a number of outer garments to choose from. The pelisse continued to be a fashionable top coat until about 1830. It was cut on the same lines as a dress and reached the ankles. It might be lined or not, depending on the time of year. Cloaks or mantles were either three-quarter or full length. Winter cloaks were lined with fur. The *witzchoura* mantle, a fashion from Poland, was three-quarter length and had either a long cape or wide, open sleeves. Evening cloaks were sometimes lined and trimmed with swansdown. Other outdoor garments were the shawl and the burnouse. The latter was a large, hooded evening cloak based on the Egyptian styles that became popular, after Napoleon's Egyptian campaign.

Hats

Between the years eighteen-fifteen and eighteen-forty women's hats, for indoors and out, became more and more elaborate. The early indoor hats were simple caps of fine lawn trimmed with lace. Before long the trimmings began to get more complicated, and ribbons and sometimes artificial flowers were added. Berets and turbans were the favourites for the evening. They too were trimmed with ribbons and were often enormous. One plaintive writer, seated for dinner between two ladies who were wearing berets, complained that he had only "an occasional glimpse of his plate." Headgear for outdoors was no less exaggerated. Straw hats from Leghorn or Dunstable were loaded with decoration. Silk or satin bonnets with huge brims acted as bases for whole gardens of flowers. The ribbons that were used to hold the bonnets on the head were sometimes trimmed with pleated tulle or lace. This gave the effect of a little ruff, called a *mentonnière,* under the chin.

The simple Greek styles of the turn of the century were now augmented with enormous quantities of false hair, plaited, curled and arranged in chignons. Ringlets were allowed to fall over the ears, or the hair might be twisted into a tight roll and pinned on the top of the head in an "Apollo" knot. In the evening these knots would be supported by tortoiseshell or ivory combs and trimmed with ribbon, flowers, jewels or "glauvina" pins, with metal knobs at the end. Men's hair was still kept short, though poorer people might allow theirs to grow, and there was a fashion for whiskers meeting under the chin.

Casual Wear

A gentleman in the eighteen-twenties, with nothing better to do than decide what to wear, could hardly get by without changing three or four times a day. His first outfit, for breakfast—which was probably none too early—consisted of a dressing gown and loose trousers in patterned chintz, worn with an open necked shirt. A coloured scarf might be knotted carelessly around his neck, and slippers *à la Chinese* or in vaguely Turkish style were worn. The outfit was completed by a tasselled "Greek" stocking cap, made fashionable by Lord Byron.

Accessories

Men carried "quizzing-glasses", single eye-glasses on short stems through which they could gaze enquiringly at anything that took their interest. Sometimes these glasses would be set in the tops of canes or walking-sticks. Ebony or blackthorn canes with ivory or gold tops were carried. They were usually trimmed with tassels. Beau Brummel put aside his cane in wet weather and carried a brown silk umbrella which, when not in use, was protected by a matching cover.

Soldier's hat, or shako, of the Chasseurs d'Afrique c. 1840

Little girl wearing mantelet

Sun bonnet 1823

Man in tall top hat, side whiskers, and quizzing glass c. 1840

Sun bonnet 1836

Sun, or poke, bonnet with country flower decoration

Lady's top hat with trailing veil 1834

Young lady wearing coat with loose sleeves 1836

ostrich feathers

Young girl in outdoor clothes 1822

Young man in outdoor clothes 1827

white satin bonnet

gold braid

high collar

checked cravat

very high, ruffled and pleated muslin collar

cotton percale dress

yellow waistcoat

embroidered spencer jacket

puffed shoulders

long velour sleeves

blue and green shawl

green waisted coat

shirt with pleated cuffs

top hat

white pantaloons

muslin flounces

white socks

pink satin shoes with ribbon

straps under feet

low-cut leather shoes with bow

The Frenchman invented the ruffle, the Englishman added the shirt.

Ralph Waldo Emerson (1803-1882)

Straw bonnet with ribbons c. 1820

Cravat in the *primo tempo* style 1830

The Crinoline

Crinoline 1862

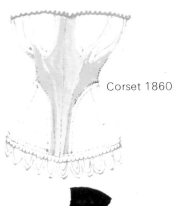

Corset 1860

From eighteen-forty until about eighteen-seventy a woman's outline was determined by that fashion, which, more than any other, is associated with the Victorian era: the crinoline. This cage to hold out the skirts began in a fairly modest way as a stiffened, horsehair petticoat. By the time it reached its extreme shape it had become a favourite subject for cartoonists. It was not confined to wealthy members of the fashionable upper classes, and because it was a comparatively cheap garment it was even worn by girls working in the fields, where it must have been very inconvenient.

One of the basic undergarments for women was a shift made of cotton or lawn, decorated with lace or embroidery according to the means of the wearer. With the shift was worn a pair of long drawers of the same material, also lace-trimmed, perhaps with ribbons threaded through. The corset became more and more restricting, and was worn on top of the shift. It reached from over the bosom to the bottom of the stomach and was laced very tightly down the back. It has been described

as "that inevitable ruin to life and beauty." Ladies determined to be smart were not deterred, and laced themselves into corsets with whalebone, wood or metal panels down the front, and with additional whalebone supports in the sides. Then one or two petticoats were put on, and over them the crinoline, which might be one of various kinds.

The most popular, because it it was the cheapest, was made of sprung steel. The "Thompson" crinoline was lightest of all, and was worn by those ladies who could afford it. An invention which seemed a good idea until put into practice was a crinoline of inflatable rubber tubes, which could be increased or decreased in size at will. This failed to catch on because of a tendency to puncture. Most crinolines opened up the front, to allow the wearer to put them on, and tied round the waist. They could be round or oval, and varied in size from the reasonable to the enormous. A contemporary cartoon shows a fashionable couple coming downstairs, with the man walking on the outside of the banisters because his lady's skirt occupies the whole width

of the staircase. At the height of the fashion skirts measured as much as two metres across. Even the women who chose not to wear a crinoline had extremely wide skirts, held by an enormous number of petticoats.

The luxury of the Second Empire in France, and the prosperity of Victorian England encouraged the wearing of elaborate dresses. One of the world's great dressmakers, the Englishman, Charles Frederick Worth, opened a workshop in Paris and managed to attract the attention of the Empress Eugénie. He introduced a style which, at first, the Empress thought too daring: a skirt and jacket, worn with a high-necked blouse. This outfit was the first version of what nowadays is a tailored suit.

Dresses were usually made in two parts, the bodice and the skirt. There were different styles of bodices for day and evening wear. The evening neckline was low, whereas that for the day was high.

One of the most popular styles was the jacket bodice. The top fitted tightly and the skirt was either short or long. Sometimes these jackets were worn open

Frock coat, necktie,
broad stripe on trousers,
1857

Lady in "capote" hat tied under
chin, crinoline dress with ruffled
white undersleeves, France 1852

Bowler hat, English   Bowler hat, French

Lady's evening lace
sleeve 1855

over waistcoats, although this style was thought to be a little too sporting for very respectable women. The bodice could also be made with a false waistcoat front, which for some reason was thought more seemly. Sleeves on day dresses were always wide and open, and reached three-quarters of the way down the arm. It was necessary, therefore, to wear false sleeves, called *engageantes*. These might be made of the same material as the bodice, but were more usually of white muslin or linen. Day dresses had their share of trimming. Braid and fringe were popular, and buttons on waistcoats could be very decorative.

In the evening, lace and embroidery came into their own and the huge skirts were covered with flounces, ribbons and posies of very natural-looking artificial flowers. The evening bodice, which was sometimes worn with a daytime skirt, was nearly always pointed at the waist in front, and often in the back as well. The neckline was extremely low, though it could be trimmed with a deep lace collar, or "bertha". The tiny sleeves were hidden by this

collar or by pleated material that matched the rest of the dress.

The correct riding dress for ladies was carefully laid down. Trousers made of chamois leather were "indispensable to modesty and comfort," according to a book on the riding habit. These were covered with the same material as the habit from knee to foot, because pale coloured trousers would catch the eye of the spectator if the habit flew up. Kid or leather boots were recommended, but too much underclothing was discouraged. A quilted black satin or silk petticoat was suggested as ideal, since it held out the skirt of the habit without attracting attention as a white one might. A habit-shirt was worn, made of white linen, with a small, turn-over collar. The jacket could have either tight or wide sleeves. In the latter case, it would be necessary to have undersleeves either of the same material as the habit or of linen like the shirt. The correct position of the waist of the jacket was shorter than in ordinary attire, and the jacket itself was made to fit closely over the bust. A well-cut and beautifully made

habit was said to improve a moderately good figure.

Men's clothes were gradually developing into the styles which are familiar today. Trousers were wider, and no longer held under the feet with straps. Short jackets were now worn both for business and relaxation. Knickerbockers were popular for wearing in the country. Clothes in general fitted more loosely than they did in the past.

The "Tweedside" lounge suit had a fairly long jacket that reached halfway down the thighs, and matching waistcoat and trousers. The edges of the jacket, the pockets and sleeves were usually bound with ribbon. By 1860 most men wore turn-down collars during the day, with cravats or neckties very like modern ones. For the evening, stand-up collars were preferred, and it was not for some time that the points were turned over into the modern butterfly shape. The forerunner of the modern morning coat was the "shooting" coat. It buttoned tight over the chest and was cut away in an inverted V from the waist. The tails finished just behind the knee.

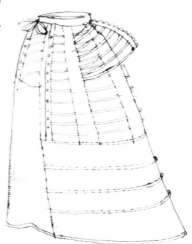

"Crinolette" of 1873 with
extra frame for bustle

Tie-on bustle to go on
top of crinoline

1865—seaside dress with
mantle, straw hat, muslin veil

French workman 1848

French infantryman 1850; his
hat is a tall "shako"

91

Bonnets

Most women wore small caps indoors, though, by the eighteen-fifties, they were going out of style for unmarried women. Bonnets were worn almost universally. They varied in size from the large-brimmed, fringed straw bonnet, covered with ostrich feathers and trimmed with pink roses, which Queen Victoria wore in 1840, to the tiny, Empire bonnet of 1865, which hardly covered the back of the head. It was not until about 1870 that bonnets were replaced by hats. Even then a hat was thought too informal for wearing to church. In bright sunshine, particularly at the seaside, a pleated and stiffened silk shade called an "Ugly" could be tied over the brim of the bonnet to shield the eyes. Hats were fashionable for riding. A version of a man's top hat was popular, as was a low crowned hat with a wide brim, often trimmed with an ostrich feather. Veils were worn, but were kept short on riding hats.

Bonnet, 1840, trimmed inside and out

White "chip" straw hat, trimmed with velvet

Lace capote with ostrich plume

Jewellery and Accessories

Men wore a good deal of jewellery at this time, if they could afford it. Signet rings, watch chains, tie pins with carved or jewelled heads and ornamental buttons on waistcoats were all worn during the day. Gold or jewelled shirt studs and cufflinks were worn in the evening. Monocles were very fashionable, and required a great deal of practice. Umbrellas and light canes were carried. Gloves were short and very plain. Women also carried umbrellas and parasols, sometimes the very tiny silk ones that were introduced in 1858, and known as "Telegram parasols". They often had handles carved from ivory or coral. Women wore bracelets, sometimes two on the same arm, and towards the end of the period heavy necklaces were worn with evening dress.

Mantles and Pelisses

The most popular overcoat for women was known variously as the mantle, the pelisse, the pardessus or the pelisse-mantle. The length was the same—about halfway down the skirt. The mantle was collarless. It had a full back, but was fitted to the waist in front, and was usually trimmed with ribbon. The pelisse was fitted to the waist all round, and might be trimmed with fur. The pelisse-mantle was completely unwaisted. It was double breasted with a wide, flat collar, and had pockets low down in the front. All these overcoats had wide sleeves to cover those of the dresses beneath.

Hair and Beards

Throughout these thirty years women's hair was parted in the middle. In the eighteen-forties curls were allowed to hang down on either side of the face. These curls were often false and it was possible to buy a complete set, with a convincing parting, which lay right across the front of the head. By the fifties, side curls were not seen so often. The hair was dressed to the back of the head and arranged in a bun, from which some curls might be allowed to stray in the evening. Men's hair, which was parted at the side in the forties, had a centre parting by the mid-fifties. Full side-whiskers were popular, and moustaches became fashionable at the time of the Crimean War. In 1861, an actor called E A Sothern played the part of Lord Dundreary in a play by Tom Taylor. The immense side whiskers that Sothern wore in the role became enormously fashionable.

Huge side-whiskers, starched cravat c. 1850

Lady's mantle coat 1852

Materials

Broadcloth, a woollen material so-called because it was originally woven double width, was used for men's coats and ladies' riding habits. Something called "cachmerette", which was lighter, was used in summer. Silk was used for evening waistcoats and for facing the lapels of formal coats, but daytime waistcoats were of cashmere, wool or heavy cotton. Women's day dresses were often made of cotton. Check gingham was cheap and, therefore, popular; and fine muslin, known as "book" muslin, was thought proper for young girls. Book muslin was even used for wedding dresses in the eighteen-sixties. Warmer clothes were made of wool, camelhair, flannel or serge. Broadcloth might be used for winter overcoats. Evening dresses were of satin or silk taffeta, velvet or brocade. The lace from Brussels, Honiton or Chantilly was used in great profusion as decoration.

Wedding Dresses

It was usual to wear a wedding dress in the style of the day, made from white silk or satin and heavily trimmed with lace. Brussels lace was particularly popular. The same material was used for the veil, which did not cover the face, but hung down the back, fixed to the hair with a circle of orange blossom. If a veil was not worn, the bride might wear a white satin bonnet, decorated with orange blossom and white ribbons. It was not until the late eighteen-sixties that the veil began to be worn over the face.

Here comes the bride—dress we now think "regular"

high stiff collar, black cravat

dark purple frock coat

checked waistcoat

tight trousers, broad stripe

top hat, gloves

underfoot straps

fan with tassel

decorative cap, worn indoors

1857—pelerine jacket with slit sleeves undersleeves trimmed to match cap

Muslin "braces" 1855

Fashion is like God; man cannot see into its holy of holies and live.

Samuel Butler (1817-1862)

Morning fichu 1855

The American Civil War

Union Cavalry, grey coat, armed with sabre

Officer's cap
Confederate State
Artillery, 1860

The American Civil War was fought from mid-1861, when the first Battle of Bull Run took place, to the surrender of the Confederate Army, May 26, 1865. The names of battles, Shiloh, Fredericksburg, Gettysburg and Missionary Ridge have gone down in history as have the names of some of the men involved in the war, Abraham Lincoln, and Generals Grant, Sherman, and "Stonewall" Jackson.

The economy of the South relied very heavily on the labour of imported black slaves, and the interference of Congress, in the North, was deeply resented. As far back as 1808 Congress had prohibited the importation of slaves. Discontent with the way things were going led to the secession of South Carolina from the Union on December 20, 1860. Six more Southern States followed suit in January and February, 1861. Four Border States seceded in April and May of the same year, and on July 21, 1861, the Union troops of the North met Jackson's Confederate troops outside Washington, where the Union troops were forced to retreat. Many historians believe that in spite of their early success, the Southern troops were bound to lose in the long run, as the population of the North was more than twice that of the South, and the South lacked the North's industrial power.

Of the nine million population of the South, three and a half million were Negroes, and slave trading was very big business. William Russell, a correspondent for the London *Times*, described a slave sale. He wrote of a slave wearing a broad, greasy "wide-awake" hat, a blue jacket, a coarse cotton shirt, loose and rather ragged "trowsers", and broken leather shoes. A woman slave was described as looking "pretty much like a London servant girl," with shoes which were mere shreds of leather, and a very battered bonnet.

Not all slaves were harshly treated, and many became trusted members of their owners' households. A butler wore a blue, swallow-tailed coat of broadcloth with big, brass buttons. A visitor to the South described his host's women servants as being "so well dressed that Solomon in all his glory might find a new proverb." One mistress of a large house in North Carolina made all her servants' clothes. Every year she gave each woman a thick dress, chemise, shoes and a blanket. The men were provided with pantaloons and jacket, a shirt, shoes and a blanket, with caps for themselves and bonnets for their wives. Great unhappiness was caused when these big estates were sold, for the slave families were often bought by different owners and separated from each other.

The soldiers on both sides at first expected the war to be over quickly. Uniforms were very informal to begin with. In the ranks any kind of coat might be worn with a shirt and pantaloons, and a cap, straw hat, or no hat at all. One observer pointed out that this was the ideal outfit for the steamy Southern climate in summer. By November, 1861, when all the winter clothes had been handed out, the army presented a more uniform appearance. The Washington artillery was recruited from the leading families in New Orleans and wore light blue uniforms. The New Orleans

Southern slave

Southern country man,
not aiming at fashion

Southern gentleman
top hat,
frilled shirt, under-
strapped pantaloons

1865: Lady's morning cap, muslin

Corset 1865

Trimming for a dinner dress 1868

CS cavalry trooper, felt hat, armed with sabre

Zouaves had blue-braided jackets, trousers, striped with light grey and red, and red caps. According to one writer, the young men carried dress suits with them, and nearly every soldier had a servant, and "a whole lot of forks and spoons." Their sisters and fiancées gave them embroidered slippers, pin-cushions and needlebooks, so that they would be able to live as comfortably and elegantly as possible.

The Union army of the North was assembled with remarkable speed. According to one English observer, it was well equipped, with clothing that was substantial and fitted easily. That, however, was not the experience of one of the recruits. He wrote home that his trousers were three or four inches too long, and his flannel shirt was coarse and un-pleasant—too large at the neck and too small everywhere else. His forage cap was an ungainly bag with a cardboard top and a leather visor, and his greatcoat was far too big for him. Only his jacket fitted. His sister had given him a "housewife", a folder of leather or cloth which contained needles, pins, thread,

buttons and scissors, and during the weeks following his enlist-ment he cut down his uniform "so that he could see out of it." Some of the individual regiments were rather smarter, such as the 1st Battalion of Rifles, which wore dark green uniforms, trimmed with light green.

Civilian clothing was very like that worn in London or Paris. The South had been influenced more by France and the North by England. The styles were several years out of date, by the standards of those centres of of fashion, but were as close to the latest ideas as could be managed. In the South, which was a more rural area, tastes changed more slowly. Men were still wearing pantaloons that strapped under the foot, frilled shirts and high collars with cravats. Embroidered waistcoats and silk-faced frock coats were also regular wear. Colours were much lighter and more summery than those worn else-where.

The most important raw material produced by the South, used by North and South alike, was cotton. The anti-slavery writer, David Christy, coined the

phrase "Cotton is King".

Cotton was used for a variety of materials, check ginghams, muslins, tarlatans, piqué and cotton-backed satin among them. Percale and dimity were used for summer dresses. Dimity was strong enough to be made into curtains and bed hangings. Calico was one of the cheapest cotton materials. Five metres were enough to make a dress for a woman in the rural South. In the smallest communities the purchase of a calico dress was something to be talked about, as most women used to wear a plain skirt and shirt for everyday.

At the height of the war, in 1863, materials became very scarce and wives and sisters in the South had to turn their hands to all kinds of skills. In Leon County, Florida, one girl spun wool into knitting yarn and knitted vests and drawers for her soldier brother, who had written to say that his underwear was in shreds.

Clippings of lambs' wool were spun into knitting yarn, and this was dyed various colours. An early method of tie-dyeing was practised.

Full dress hat, infantry sergeant, Union Army

Union statesman; sober colours, long waistcoat

Lady in crinoline with lace-trimmed matching cap.

Lieut-Gen. of Union Army; gold cords on hat

Rank chevrons of QMS, CS Army

Bonnets and Hats

No matter how serious the fighting, some sort of head covering was thought essential. The men wore hats for protection, or because they were regulation army issue. The women wore bonnets because it was improper to go out without one. In 1865, the last year of the war, one Southern girl paid two hundred dollars in the devalued Confederate currency for a new bonnet, so important was it to her outfit. In the big cities it was still possible to copy European styles, but when the war was at its fiercest in the South all sorts of makeshift headgear was invented. In 1862 the Confederate supporters were still optimistic, and declared that if a man's hat of wheaten straw could be made by his wife in three days, they were quite self-sufficient. The dried fronds of the dwarf palm were plaited and sewn into the shape of a hat. It was then pressed on a hat-block if anyone had the necessary skill. A ribbon around the crown finished off an acceptable hat for a boy going back to school. A form of marrow, known as the "bonnet squash", or "Spanish dish-rag", was grown. Its fibres were dried and made into hats. Women used to make wire frames for bonnets, which they covered with scraps of material or even paper and then trimmed with goose or chicken feathers, dyed with the juice of berries or indigo mud.

Jewellery

High-necked dresses were worn during the day and, therefore, women did not care for elaborate necklaces. They contented themselves with a small brooch at the throat, sometimes decorated with a miniature portrait. Earrings were worn, varying from small gold or turquoise studs in pierced ears to long, dangling shapes on fine chains. Semi-precious stones such as agate or cairngorm were popular. Cheap versions of fashionable brooches could be bought, made out of imitation gold, or "pinchbeck". The lower evening necklines encouraged the use of lockets hung on chains or ribbons, with a picture of a loved one inside, or even a lock of hair, carefully plaited and preserved under glass. Gold or silver watches were worn. They were hung from the shoulder on chains and pinned to the waist or the breast. Mourning jewellery was made of jet, cut steel, or "marquesite", or a wrinkled black stone called "crêpe stone".

Accessories for Travel

Travelling was becoming much easier by this time. The railways had improved, particularly in the North, and travelling equipment was carefully designed and chosen. Ladies carried their indoor caps in "band-boxes", descendants of the containers in which Elizabethan ruffs had been sent to and from the laundry. Cardboard hat boxes were usually supplied by the milliner who made the hats, but men had to provide their own leather hat boxes for their journeys. Carpet bags were popular and useful to both sexes. For longer trips clothes might be packed in wooden chests, covered with cow-hide and decorated with brass nails.

Aprons

Nearly every woman, whatever her class, wore an apron at some time during the day. The smallest and least useful were worn by fashionable housewives, and were so tiny that they were known as "fig-leaves". They were usually made of black silk or satin, and trimmed with black lace. It was customary for these ladies to wear rather larger aprons when they were doing needlework of any kind, to prevent the loose threads falling on their dresses. Housemaids wore large, white cotton aprons in the morning and smaller, lawn ones in the afternoon, when tea was served. Cooks wore aprons of check gingham. Schoolteachers and shop assistants wore black cotton aprons, very often with matching false sleeves to protect their cuffs.

Fans

The smart women in the big cities had no intention of letting the war upset their lives more than was necessary, and assemblies and balls were enthusiastically attended. Fans were carried in the evening by all well-dressed women, and were made of silk, gauze or linen, on ivory, coral or sandalwood sticks. Mother-of-pearl sticks were popular on fabric fans which had been stuck with spangles. These fans were quite small, but larger, plumed fans were becoming popular for dances.

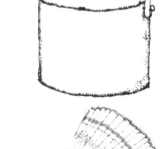

Lady's hatbox

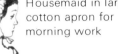

Gentlemen's leather top-hat case

Union cavalry officer's hat

Ostrich plumes and long veil 1865

Velvet bonnet c. 1859

Man's top hat 1851

Southern straw hat as worn by slaves

Printer—long apron, black false sleeves to protect shirt

Fan with ivory sticks

Housemaid in large cotton apron for morning work

Lady's costume 1866

red képi with regt. number

Uniform of the 14th Brooklyn NY State militia Zouave style

cord epaulettes

hort jacket, red vaistcoat, silver uttons

eather belt with State of New York uckle

gy pantaloons ked into gaiters

canvas gaiters

morning cap

mantle trimmed with lace and braid

white silk dress, ribbon trimmings

Cavalry officer's leather gauntlet glove

It is an interesting question how far men would retain their relative rank if they were divested of their clothes.

Henry David Thoreau (1817-1894)

Straw hat for a little girl c. 1860

97

The Bustle

Ribbon and
flower headdress
1872

Tailcoat, light
waistcoat, top hat
for evening wear

After the crinoline had reached its extreme width it went out of fashion and the huge skirts again changed shape. The bustle, an undergarment which allowed the front of the skirt to lie flat while extending the back of it, made a brief appearance in the late eighteen-sixties. The dress was pulled into shape by tapes that were sewn under the skirt and tied back.

Another style that was popular was the "Dolly Varden" dress, named after the character in Charles Dickens' novel *Barnaby Rudge*. It was of printed material, usually chintz, with sleeves and neckline of a vaguely Georgian character. It was worn over a skirt of plain colour. The skirt of the top dress was lifted in front and gathered into an enormous bunch of material at the back. A simple straw has was worn with this fashion, and the hair was arranged in "shepherdess" ringlets.

By the middle of the eighteen-seventies, however, the bustle had disappeared again, and skirts were tight all the way down. Sometimes they were so tight that women could hardly move their feet more than fifteen

centimetres at a time. These very narrow skirts often had long trains, which swept the ground.

Women used a good many artificial aids to improve their shapes for the tight dresses. A French magazine showed a series of satirical drawings of false bosoms, behinds, calves and thighs, and even false stomachs. A rubber false behind, the magazine suggested, was very practical if one should fall over when skating, but care should be taken that it did not puncture. Though the magazine's intention was humorous, all these appliances were actually available in some form or other.

The vogue for slim, tight dresses lasted until about 1883 when the bustle reappeared, in a much more exaggerated shape than before. It consisted of a straw-filled cushion that was sewn into the skirt, and a series of steel half-loops that were inserted into the lining of the back of the skirt, to hold the shape all the way to the ground. Tight-laced corsets were still thought essential, and in some cases even beneficial, though it is difficult to imagine what benefits could be gained from

such constriction of the waist and the rib cage.

Dresses were usually made with the bodice and skirt separate. The skirt very often was draped to make it look as if there was an overskirt as well. There were several different styles of bodice. The very plain, high necked one usually fastened at the back or in front. Another bodice was cut rather in the shape of a coat, often on masculine lines with short coat-tails and two buttons at the hip.

A very great influence on clothes at this time was the international success of Mr. Singer's famous sewing machine. The fact that clothing could now be made economically by machines led to the opening of the first big department stores, such as *Wanamaker's* in Philadelphia, *La Samaritaine* and *Printemps* in Paris, and *Liberty's* in London. In these stores women could, for the first time, buy ready-made dresses, cheap machine-made stockings, and shoes and hats which they could take away with them, rather than having to wait days, or sometimes weeks for the milliner or shoemaker to com-

Afternoon dress and child's
simple day dress

Young girl and lady in outdoor
summer dress with parasol,
France 1887

Hat with broad
band, narrow brim
Paris 1885

Straw hat,
France 1876

Boy in sailor suit
acting as ball boy

plete the work. It was no longer necessary to agree the price of a garment with its maker, all the articles in the big stores were marked with their prices, and shopping to be smart became much simpler.

Although 1880 to 1890 was a period of economic depression in Europe, the wealthy managed to dress very sumptuously. Cheaper materials, which imitated the costly ones at a fraction of the price, were used more frequently. No matter how luxurious a dress might look at first sight, the price of it could well have been reduced by the use of cheap lining materials. Poorer quality fabrics were used in parts of the garment which did not show. Velveteen and sateen were popular for cheaper, ready-made dresses, and there was a material called "plushette", which was made into pelisses and cloaks.

The increased interest that women took in sports, such as tennis, archery and tricycling, made false hair unfashionable for a while. Hair was brushed back into a bun, which might be placed on the nape of the neck, higher up the head, or even on top. The front hair was usually

arranged in a fringe, either crimped or straight depending on the wearer's taste. Towards the end of the decade women began to brush their fringes back over pads of cotton wool or false hair, a style which led to the hair fashions of the early part of the next century.

Men's clothes continued to get more and more like those we know today. There were two types of frock coat. The everyday one, which buttoned high on the chest, was increasingly popular for business wear. The dress frock coat had only two pairs of buttons and, usually, a velvet collar with silk lapels. This was worn for formal occasions during the day, but by the end of the eighteen-seventies had more or less gone out of fashion and was replaced by the morning coat. This also had two styles. One was very similar to the riding coat of the early part of the century, and the other was rather longer, with a high, turn-over collar which buttoned up to the neck. Short jackets, usually for more casual occasions, were now worn by quite a few men.

Men wore trousers that were still quite wide. Pantaloons,

however, had gone completely out of style. It had been the custom in bad weather to turn up the bottoms of the trousers, and in the middle of the eighteen-eighties very smart young men, known as "Mashers", would wear turn-ups regardless of the weather. Thus began a masculine style which has gone in and out of fashion ever since.

An outfit that came into favour was the "Norfolk" suit, made from check tweed. The jacket was belted either all the way round or just at the back. It was worn with knickerbockers, knitted woollen stockings and boots. This was thought suitable for all kinds of country pursuits.

Gentlemen indulged in a great many sports and wore different outfits for each one. For shooting there was a version of the morning coat, made with capacious pockets and leather patches on the shoulders. For leisurely yachting a suit of white flannel or duck was worn, with a casual shirt and a loosely knotted tie. An alternative to a white jacket was a reefer coat in blue serge. Cricket was played in white flannels.

French cartoon showing
figure "improvements"

White tennis dress,
skirt pinned up

Dressed for tennis 1883

France 1884 : opera
costume

Tennis Wear

Lawn tennis was all the rage, and to play it women wore special dresses. It was far from the energetic game which we know now, and no lady would think of leaving off her corset in order to take part. The dresses were made on the same lines as the ordinary day dresses of the period, though they had less trimming, and were provided with an arrangement of hooks and eyes so that the skirt could be drawn up a little in front. Short trains were quite customary. Some women wore little aprons with pockets in them to hold the tennis balls, and some wore dresses with pockets large enough to hold the racquet while refreshments were being taken. Black stockings and shoes, to be as inconspicuous as possible, were worn. The shoes had black rubber soles. Gloves and plain straw hats were recommended.

Evening Dresses

Until the middle of the eighteen-eighties evening dresses were of a style similar to those worn during the day, but they were covered with as much trimming as possible. Flowers, lace, bows, fringe, swagged or pleated silk were all used. If it was possible to trim the trimming, that was done as well. Artificial pearls and sequins were sewn on, and feathers or even whole birds were attached to any empty space. The hem of the skirt and the very long train were trimmed with a deep frill of gauze or stiff lace known as a *balayeuse*. It was usual to have a silken cord loop attached to the skirt, which might be put over the wrist to hold the train out of the way while dancing. Towards the end of the decade there was a fashion for sleeveless, low-cut bodices, which caused a certain amount of scandalized comment.

Materials and Colours

Men had a good variety of materials to choose from, with check tweed being one of the most popular for casual wear. Checks and stripes at the time tended to be rather larger than is customary now, and some young men went even further and wore very "noisy" clothes, of which a fashion magazine said the patterns were "more striking than tasteful." In general, there were few lightweight fabrics for men, though twill, which was also called "diagonal" because it was made in such a way that it gave a diagonal pattern to the cloth, could be woven almost as fine as cashmere for summer coats. Paisley patterned wool might be used for dressing gowns, and velvet was popular for "breakfast", or "smoking", jackets. Women were able to buy dresses in an enormous range of fabrics. Wool, and silk and wool mixture were popular during the day, and silk, satin and velvet in the evening. The colours of some of the dresses were very strong, as aniline dyes had been invented in the eighteen-fifties. Electric blue, canary yellow and magenta were often combined with black for a fashionable outfit.

Trimmings

It is difficult to think of a small animal or insect that was not used, either real or imitation, to decorate a dress or hat. Feathers and birds were used to trim hats, and white doves' wings were thought very smart when attached to the hair. There was a huge importation business in dead birds. As many as thirty thousand were sold at auction in one afternoon. Dresses might have trimmings of cats' heads, or three or four mice running up the skirt, and moths, butterflies and many other insects were all to be found adorning the well-dressed woman.

Rational Dress

There was, naturally enough, a reaction against the expensive and constricting fashions of the time, and societies to promote rational dress were formed. Men wore Norfolk suits with deer-stalker hats, casual shirts open at the neck and thick hand-knitted woollen stockings. Women's clothes were much simpler than was fashionable, and the divided-skirt dress was very popular, though so much material was used that the two legs looked as if they formed an ordinary skirt. Some more daring women wore "Turkish" trousers and long flowing coats at home.

Aesthetic Dress

In the eighteen-eighties artists, poets and other writers were very influenced by the paintings of Edward Burne-Jones, who produced imaginary and idealized scenes of mediaeval life. Another influence was the painter and designer William Morris. He and the architect C F A Voysey designed houses together right down to the last detail, including wallpaper and curtains. A style of dress to suit these surroundings was worked out. The women wore loose gowns of wool or Liberty silk. The front of the bodice was smocked and the skirt hand-embroidered with "aesthetic" flowers, daffodils, sunflowers and so on. Popular colours were sage-green, peacock blue and terracotta.

Tennis dress with racket 1885

Pink silk evening dress with red ribbons 1873

Norfolk jacket c. 1870

"Trianon" poke bonnet, black velvet with "tropical bird" in dyed feathers 1879

1888 France

white shirt with stiff collar, bow tie

k morning jacket

rned silk tcoat

e leather gloves

ey top hat

ng stick

striped ousers

sleeveless top

long white tight-fitting gloves, gold bracelets

bustle dress with complex ribbon decorations

decoration of artificial roses

matching fan

Lingerie fichu 1872

The timid darling lady had on a most lovely sky blue coloured dress with a high bustle, and it was blossomed all over with sham daisies tied on with green ribbon.

Daisy Ashford: Love and Marriage (c. 1900)

Brown leather shoe with jet beads 1868

101

The Pioneer and the Indian

While life in New York, Washington and Boston during the nineteenth century was as near to that of the major European cities as the inhabitants could manage, prosperity came much later to other parts of America. The little town of Yerba Buena, for example, which was taken over from Mexico by the United States in 1846 and re-christened San Francisco, was a frontier town with a population of less than two hundred and fifty. On January 24, 1848, however, a worker at a new saw mill on the American River found a few flakes of gold in the tail race of the mill, and the Gold Rush was on. By May the fever was so strong that shop owners found it more profitable to close their stores and go to the gold fields themselves. The wisest ones took their stock with them, to exchange with the diggers for gold dust.

The news of California's fabulous riches travelled over the world very quickly, and prospectors converged overland by covered wagons or by sea via Panama or Cape Horn. Seagoing travellers were advised that "the light clothing, such as

Short skirt for dirt roads in mining towns

is worn in the United States during the summer months, is all sufficient for travelling purposes, from three days out of New York to within five or six days short of San Francisco, after which the usual warm clothing will be necessary." For women this meant several petticoats and a wool dress, a pelisse and a bonnet.

It was a predominantly male society in San Francisco at this time, however. Unmarried men with no home ties arrived in their thousands, and very often the only female company was provided by the hostesses in the bars. A cynical observer wrote: "There are also some honest women in San Francisco, but not very many." Many of the hostesses pretended to set up as dressmakers, milliners or collar makers. There were bona fide dressmakers, of course, as the girls in the bars needed new dresses. The styles were chosen from magazines brought into town by immigrants from other parts of the States or from abroad, and consequently were a year or two out of date.

Any man who was particular about the state of his clothes

had a great deal of trouble finding a woman to wash and iron his linen, and one bachelor married a rather plain spinster so that he could have a clean shirt every day.

Once out on the gold fields such preoccupations with cleanliness were forgotten, and men wore the toughest clothes they had. Shirts were made of canvas, calico or wool, with or without collars attached. Sturdy trousers of serge or thick cotton cloth were worn with high boots to discourage the snakes. Heavy woollen jackets were needed for nights spent in tents or rough wooden shacks. The boots, in fact, were also useful in town since there were no sidewalks in San Francisco in 1840. One observor wrote that the custom of tucking the trousers into the tops of the boots was so widespread that the days of knee breeches might have been coming back. Women were obliged to turn up the hems of their dresses to keep them out of the mud.

The prospectors who travelled overland often brought their entire families with them, hoping to establish a new life when they had staked their claim. They

Printer at work

Trail boss in fringed buckskin suit c. 1860

Miner in corduroy trousers, collarless shirt, gun in holster

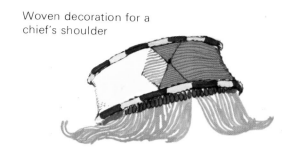
Woven decoration for a chief's shoulder

Blackfoot medicine man, magical face markings

had many dangers on their journeys but the one they feared most was an attack by Indians. The Apache. the Sioux, the Cheyenne, the Blackfoot and the Crow Indians were among the many that the covered wagon trains encountered. Some tribes were more warlike than others.

Each tribe had its individual way of dressing, which depended very much on its traditions and the climate. In mild weather, and when going about everyday tasks in times of peace, a young man would probably wear no more than a loincloth. Ceremonial clothes and winter wear were much more elaborate. One of the most usual materials for making into trousers and shirts was buckskin, the hide of the whitetail deer. This was sewn up with threads made from buffalo sinew, using a bone needle carved from the leg bone of a deer or large bird. The shirts were usually hip length, with the hem cut into fringe, and were often beautifully decorated with porcupine quills and animal hair. The quills were dyed red and yellow, and their naturally shiny surface caught the light and gave a brilliance to the

shirt which was greatly admired. Quills were used as decoration on practically everything else as well, from furniture to war bonnets. It was not until glass beads were introduced to the Indians in the early eighteen-hundreds, and found to be easier to use than the quills, that the custom stopped.

Another source of fabric was the fibrous inner bark of trees such as cedar and elm, which was separated, twisted into threads and woven with flexible grasses into heavy cloaks and shirts. The resulting material was tough enough even for shoes.

An American Indian chief in full regalia wore buckskin trousers, perhaps with beaded leather leggings, and a buckskin war shirt. The war shirt was for show rather than for battle, and was decorated with martial designs and scalps taken from his defeated opponents. A flat, oblong panel, made of fine, polished bones strung together with beads, covered the chest.It acted not only as decoration but as protection as well.

Different tribes used different trimmings for their costumes. A leader of a successful war party

from the Crow tribe would decorate his shirt and moccasins with human hair, and a warrior who had killed his opponent with a hand weapon was allowed to trim his moccasins with wolf tails. If a brave had snatched a bow or gun from his enemy in battle he trimmed his shirt with ermine tails.

The most impressive part of any Indian chief's regalia was the head-dress. Sometimes it was made of fur and animal horns, and sometimes of feathers. Feathers, for the Indians, had the significance that heraldry had for mediaeval European knights. The type and number of feathers worn indicated a man's prowess in battle. Very often a chief would not wear all the feathers he was entitled to, but for great ceremonial occasions his head-dress of eagle feathers would form a high crown and a long tail, which fell down the back. The bonnet might also be adorned with animal horns, trimmed with a band of porcupine quills or beads, and have ermine or white weasel skins hanging from it in strips.

Outer garments were made of buffalo hide, and beaver.

Yankton Sioux with horned headgear

Saloon girl c. 1889

Warrior with war paint, looted jacket and modern automatic rifle c. 1886

Sioux chief with war bonnet, quill decorations on shirt and buckskin leggings

Hair

Among the many traditions of the American Indians, the treatment of hair held a particularly important place. Many tribes considered a completely hairless body to be beautiful, and young men would remove their facial hair by plucking it out with clam shells. The men of the Pawnee tribe shaved the sides of their heads, so that only a ridge was left along the top. This was then dressed with grease to make it look like a buffalo horn. Widows and families in mourning often cut their hair short. A child's first haircut was an occasion of great importance. The custom of scalping one's enemy was intended to prove his death, but in fact many men in battle were scalped alive, and lived to tell about it. A small patch from the crown of the head was considered sufficient to prove a scalping.

Wampum

Wampum was an arrangement of beads that conveyed a message. It could be woven into belts or hatbands, or simply into message strips. In the early days each bead was carved by hand from clam shells, then coloured and strung together in intricate patterns. The most valuable wampum was purple, carved painstakingly from a small part of the clam shell. White wampum, which was just as difficult to make, was more common because there was more white shell. When the white man arrived with metal drilling tools, wampum became less highly regarded, although it was still very complicated to make. The elaborate glass bead belts which can now be bought are the direct descendants of wampum.

Body Painting

Many tribes used body painting for battles or ceremonial occasions. The paints were made from natural ingredients: red from the earth, black from charcoal, yellow from the gall bladders of the buffalo. The pigments were mixed with animal fat, or applied dry to greased bodies. Sometimes the colours were mixed with saliva in the mouth and spat directly on to the body. Some tribes considered white to be the colour of peace, and others thought of it as the colour of fertility. The Hopi, in northern Arizona, used white for the cotton bridal dresses of their girls because it matched the flower of the squash or gourd, their symbol of fertility.

Navajo Silver Jewellery

The Navajo, a tribe of the South West, have a tradition of silver jewellery dating back from the middle of the nineteenth century, when the art was taught to them by Mexican *plateros*, or silversmiths. One of the easiest articles to make was the concha, a round plaque of silver which was worn on the belt, usually in pairs. Many more complicated pieces were soon made, such as buckles, bracelets, necklaces, headstalls for horses and *ketohs*, broad wrist guards that protected the wrist from the snap of the bowstring. Originally the ketoh was made of leather, but gradually the silver ornamentation increased and solid silver plaques, decorated with marks made with cold chisels and files, were fixed to the leather bands. Turquoises were often used to ornament different pieces of jewellery.

Children

An Indian girl of the Kiowa tribe, on the Great Plains, might wear as a small child a cloth dress and leather belt, both heavily decorated with the milk teeth of the elk. These were considered one of the most treasured decorations. She would have buckskin leggings and boots, with patterns on them in beads. Necklaces of polished bone and shell beads would have been worn around her neck. Most infants were carried in portable cradleboards, shaped wooden boards with a buckskin or cloth covering that was elaborately decorated and used to secure the baby. A photograph of a young Kiowa girl, taken in the eighteen-nineties, shows her holding a miniature cradleboard containing a doll with a china face, probably bought from white traders.

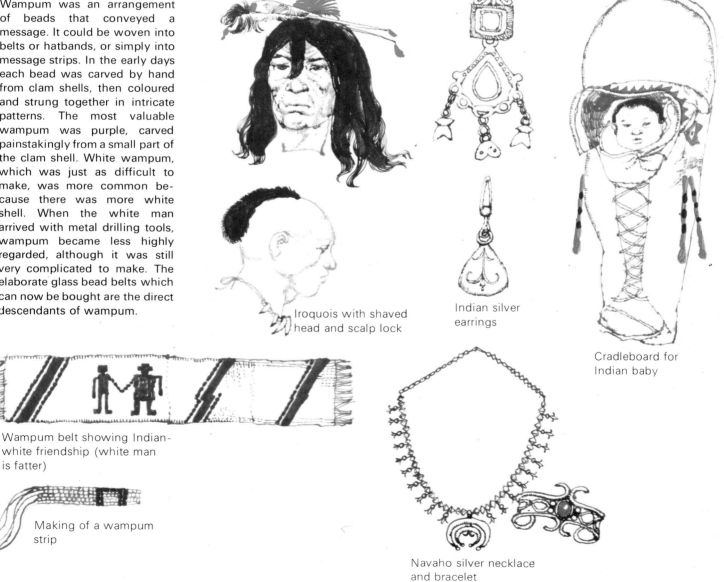

Iroquois with shaved head and scalp lock

Indian silver earrings

Cradleboard for Indian baby

Wampum belt showing Indian-white friendship (white man is fatter)

Making of a wampum strip

Navaho silver necklace and bracelet

Plains Indian brave.
Shirt is heirloom of
earlier date

Gold prospector c. 1870

red headband

felt hat

polished bone armour

Presidential medal

wool jacket, coarse
linen shirt

ceremonial
pipe

buckskin shirt,
strips of fur
and leather

rcupine quill
coration on
eves

blanket roll,
clothes
inside

buckskin leggings

belt carries
revolver,
bowie knife,
drinking pan
and water canteen

pickaxe

soft leather
moccasins with
beads

rough leather boots

Wooden headdress, a whale
with human hair added

**The things named ''pants'' in certain documents,
A word not made for gentlemen, but ''gents''.**

Oliver Wendell Holmes (1809-1894)

4-shot percussion pistol
by Darling. Rotating
barrels fired in turn

Fin de Siècle

Bathing bloomers
c 1880

Afternoon blouse
1895

By the end of the nineteenth century the advances made in the world of cheap, ready-made clothes meant that smart styles were no longer the preserve of the very rich. Particularly in the cities and towns it was important to most men and women that they dressed in something resembling the latest fashion. Styles were dictated by people who led more active lives than ever before and for fashionable women it was the last time that restricting foundation garments were worn as a matter of course.

The most important article of underclothing for women was still the corset, which was constructed to reduce the size of the waist to forty-five centimetres. The corset was worn on top of a vest or chemise, and often underneath a pair of "combinations". Professor Gustav Jaeger, from the Department of Zoology at Stuttgart University, opened a shop in Regent Street in London, in 1885, where it was possible to buy the latest in the professor's designs in hygienic underwear for both women and men. Dr Jaeger declared that the only healthy clothing was that

made from animal products— wool, hair, bone or feathers. His "sanitary" woollen underwear became popular with all classes. Combination vests and drawers, woollen socks with five toes and even "sanitary" knee-warmers were all introduced in the eighteen-eighties and worn universally by the mid-nineties.

It was, however, difficult for smart women to accommodate so much woollen material under their tight bodices, and though Dr Jaeger's designs for combinations were enthusiastically taken up, less bulky fabrics such as muslin, silk or cellular cotton were used for underwear. On top of the combinations came yet another undergarment, a pair of knickers, silk, cotton or cambric, usually trimmed with lace and ribbon. Stockings of silk, cotton lisle, or wool for winter were held up by suspenders attached to a belt round the waist.

The bustle vanished, leaving a bell-shaped skirt with a tiny waist and a very wide hem, and enormous sleeves. The outline was similar to that of the 1830s. The huge leg o' mutton sleeves were very like the sleeves of the eighteen-thirties. They reached

their extreme and then disappeared in 1896, in exactly the same way as their predecessors had done in 1836.

By far the most popular style at this time was the "tailor-made" suit, the natural successor to the jacket and skirt outfit designed by Worth in the eighteen-sixties. Greater activity by women in shops, factories and offices led to increased popularity for the blouse and skirt—to such an extent that the dressmakers complained that the blouse was putting them out of business. The easiest thing to wear over a blouse for outdoors was a short jacket. This varied in length. Some were very fitting and reached as far as the waist. They could have vast puffed sleeves. Others, if worn with a slightly shorter skirt, reached to the hips. For shooting, bicycling or walking one of the longer jackets could be worn with a skirt which reached only to the lower calf. Any suggestion of indecency was counteracted by wearing high, buttoned boots. A calf length skirt was thought unfeminine, even for the most active pastimes, and all kinds of difficulties arose when the full

From a pattern book
of November 1899

Cloth gown for
walking

Serge bathing suit
c. 1885

Canvas bathing shoe
with rope sole c. 1875

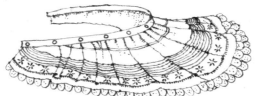

Detachable train for an
underskirt 1880

Feathered hat (from
Weldon's *Ladies' Journal*)

skirt caught the wind. This problem was solved by weighting the hem of the skirt with shot.

Skirts were cut in a number of styles, though most of them were flat in front with all the fullness of material at the back. It was no longer necessary to wear a bustle, though some skirts with large pleats were held out by fluted frames that were attached to the waist under the dress. One of the most popular of these was called *La Pliante*.

Evening dresses followed the lines of those worn during the day, though they had very low necklines and the sleeves were even more exaggerated. For less formal occasions an evening blouse and skirt might be worn. For dinners that were not followed by dancing, there were dresses with tiny jackets that finished above the waist. The dresses were made with small sleeves, or even shoulder straps. The vast, puffed sleeves were part of the jacket, which would also have very wide revers lying on top of the sleeves.

A style adapted from men's clothing, and very popular in the summer, was the "shirtwaist" dress. For informal occasions,

particularly in America, men had started to wear shirts without waistcoats, belted trousers and short jackets. Women copied this idea, and wore striped cotton shirts with high starched collars, mannish ties and skirts with belts. Even with this casual outfit, however, the sleeves still retained the *gigot* fullness.

In the evening men wore dress suits of vicuna or worsted, with shirts and waistcoats of white cotton piqué. The "Dress Lounge Jacket" was introduced, and became known as the "Dinner Jacket". It was cut on the same lines as the daytime short lounge jacket. It was not buttoned up the front so that the band of material round the waist, the forerunner of the modern cummerbund, would show. The dinner jacket was not acceptable at formal dinners or at gatherings where ladies were present. It was supposed to be reserved for informal suppers, concerts and music halls.

The morning coat was still the most usual, formal daytime wear. There was a very short-lived fashion for wearing highly coloured waistbands or cummerbunds with morning clothes,

instead of waistcoats.

More and more men wore lounge suits. There was a "morning" version of these as well, with the jacket longer than average and cut away in front from a button just above the waist, like the shooting jacket. Waistcoats were always worn with lounge suits. They were sometimes made of the same material but were often in a contrasting fabric.

A man with any sense of style wore a corset over his vest to reduce his figure. Shirts were usually of starched cotton, though increasing informality led to less frequent use of starch. Some soft fronted shirts were pleated. No matter how soft the shirt, however, the collar was always starched, except for very rustic activities. It reached its maximum height at about this time. Seven centimetres was the height considered very smart by the end of the decade. Turn-over collars were worn during the day, but in the evening only stand-up collars were permissible, with the points turned over either slightly or not at all.

Outdoor costume 1899
with fur boa and muff

Cycling outfit with
long kid gloves, cap
and stockings, France 1895

Overcoat and plumed
straw hat 1893

French gentleman c. 1899,
broad cravat, double-breasted
waistcoat

Workboxes

No lady would be without her own private workbox where, as well as sewing equipment, she could keep letters or other personal possessions. The boxes, of which fine examples had been made for years, were of wood, leather, tortoiseshell or ivory, often lacquered or inlaid with mother of pearl. The insides were fitted with spools of ivory or wood, on which was wound cotton in various colours. The boxes contained clamps, which were screwed on to the edge of the worktable to hold the fabric while it was being worked, and needlebooks, pincushions, scissors and thimbles. An ivory holder for wax was always included. Thread was drawn through the wax to coat it before it was used to sew on buttons. Smaller workboxes took on fanciful shapes, and Queen Alexandra owned one in the shape of an ivory egg in a silver cup. When it was opened it revealed the spools, pin and needle holders and the thimble carefully arranged inside.

Accessories and Jewellery

Many women carried *chatelaine* bags, silver mounted fabric pouches which contained their handkerchiefs, their bottles of Eau de Cologne—any other perfume was thought "fast"—and their card cases. A lady calling on a new acquaintance would leave an engraved card with her name, her address and the hours at which she "received"—perhaps Tuesday and Sunday afternoons. Little jewellery was worn during the day, though in the evening

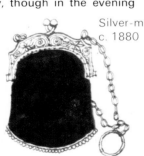
Silver-mounted chatelaine bag c. 1880

high collars of diamonds or pearls, real or fake, were worn, and black dresses might be ornamented with jet. There were three types of jet: Whitby, which was the true fossilized coal, French, which was black glass, and "composition", which was an early form of plastic and was used to reproduce cheaply the more expensive varieties.

Hats

Women's hats generally had small crowns and narrow brims, though there might be a good deal of ribbon and feather trimming around the crown. The fashion of the previous decade for fauna of various kinds had not completely gone out. Birds and small shellfish were sometimes used as trimming, and veils might be woven in spiders' web patterns. Other hats had a distinctly masculine look. The straw boater was extremely popular with shirtwaist dresses, and little felt homburg hats were often worn for bicycling. Peaked caps like those of modern schoolboys were also worn for sport. Men wore hats to suit the occasion. The silk top hat was the most formal, and the bowler or derby was a little less dressy. Bowlers were usually black though fawn or light grey were worn in the summer. Other styles included the deerstalker, the trilby and the Alpine. As women had adopted the boater, it was thought slightly effeminate for men.

Straw picture hat, trimmed roses and bows, 1894

Straw sailor hat, "Mercury" wings 1893

Bloomers

Mrs Amelia Bloomer went to England from America in 1851, and introduced her ideas on sensible clothing for women engaged in active pursuits. The garment which is most closely associated with her name was a pair of knickerbockers, "pleated at the waist and gathered into a band below the knee," also known as "rationals". When they were first introduced they were thought very daring, but by eighteen-ninety they had become accepted as permissible wear for ladies, and very smart for the sport of bicycling. Made of light, woollen fabric, they were worn with a full skirted, hip length coat with the inevitable leg o' mutton sleeves. A shirt with a starched collar, a tie, gaiters and a felt, pork-pie hat completed the outfit.

Mrs Amelia Bloomer's "reform costume"

Tennis outfit with bloomers

Haute Couture

In 1900 an exhibition of fashion was held in Paris, *Les Toilettes de la Collectivité de la Couture*, at which the great French dressmakers showed their latest models. Although it was considered quite proper to model clothes on the human form in private salons, at an exhibition it was necessary to use wax models. The styles which made French *haute couture* famous throughout the world were displayed in furnished room settings. Among the exhibitors were Worth, Paquin, Drécole, Rouff and the English dressmaker Redfern, who was famous for his tailored walking suits.

Children

Very young boys, up to the age of five or so, wore skirts. Then they were put into short trousers, which finished about the knee. European boys often wore socks that left their knees bare, but in America they were given some protection against the winter cold by long woollen stockings, which were attached to suspenders worn around the waist. Leather patches were sometimes sewn on to the knees of the stockings. The sailor suit, with its flat, turnover collar and its bloused top was popular for both boys and girls. The girls wore it with a pleated skirt, and the boys with their short trousers.

Sailor suit and laced-up boots 1897

Englishman 1890

white shirt, bow tie

short black waistcoat

black tail coat

striped trousers

velvet hat with
ostrich plumes

long white gloves

white satin dress,
France 1891

sleeves puffed to
elbow, then tight

Lady's ''toreador'' hat
1894

I'd a swallow-tail coat of a beautiful blue,
A brief that I'd bought of a booby;
A couple of shirts and a collar or two
And a ring that looked like a ruby.

W S Gilbert: Trial by Jury (1875)

Shoe of calf kid
with black leather
golosh 1893

109

Turn of the Century 1900–1914

Ribbon-trimmed straw hat c. 1906

Lady's combinations c. 1900

The Edwardian era and the twentieth century began almost simultaneously. Queen Victoria died in 1901, and was succeeded by Edward VII. So many changes in the design of women's clothes took place at the turn of the century that it virtually amounted to a fashion revolution.

In 1900, or thereabouts, the curvaceous corset of the late nineteenth century was replaced by a straight-fronted foundation, which was considered healthier than its predecessor. It pressed less heavily on the waist and allowed the wearer more freedom. Paul Poiret, the French designer started creating "walking outfits" for women, with skirts slightly above the ankle. Women wore buttoned boots with them and carried muffs.

Arthur Lasenby Liberty introduced a series of Orient-inspired patterns, which were made into softer, more flowing dresses than had been seen before. The rise of the Suffragette Movement, with its leader Mrs Emmeline Pankhurst and her slogan "Votes for Women", encouraged the wearing of clothes that were much more suitable for an active life than the formal, constricted fashions of the last years of the eighteen-hundreds.

In 1907 a lady of fashion would first put on a cotton shirt, and then her corset, an elaborately boned affair with suspenders attached for her stockings. The corsets were given all kinds of names by their manufacturers: "Cleopatra", "Enchantress", "Perdita", "Electra" (for stout figures), and cost less than £1. "Typoline", a wonderful piece of ribbon-and-lace-covered engineering, was priced at 14/6d. Women's stockings were black, white or tan. In winter they might be cashmere, but otherwise they were of silk or cotton, sometimes embroidered. D H Lawrence wrote in *Sons and Lovers* of an old lady who made her living embroidering stockings for fashionable shops, at what would seem a pittance.

A high-necked lace blouse could be worn and a long, full skirt of flannel, broad cloth or mohair, in a subdued colour; and then a matching jacket, sometimes three-quarter length, with three-quarter length cuffed sleeves. Gloves were *always* worn out of doors. There were gloves of suede, kid, doe-skin, reindeer or gazelle; gloves for cycling, driving, walking and even sleeping. A catalogue of the period advertised "Sleeping gloves, chamois leather, perforated. . . ."

Top coats for ladies came in a variety of styles, either full length or three-quarter length and were made of smooth wool fabrics or tweed. Capes were often lined with fur, and had stand-up collars. Every well-stocked wardrobe contained a raincoat, and the manufacturers went to great lengths to point out that these were, by now, "absolutely odourless". Another of the hazards of rain-proofing had been that, apart from the smell, the rubber used to perish and crumble off the cloth, but this had been corrected in 1905.

Muffs were carried in winter, often with a matching, long, fur stole. An outfit was completed by a large hat with feathers or bows or flowers, depending on the season, and sometimes even a large bird with its wings outstretched.

Men's clothes had by now settled into the formal uniformity from which they did not break until well after World War II. In

Caped travelling coat, hat tied on with scarf, carpet bag c. 1900

"Merry Widow" hat 1908

Paletot coat, b narrow trouser spats 1905

French plumed hat 1914

Exotic hat design, *Journal des Dames et des Modes* 1905

the first decade of the twentieth century, colours were black, grey, something appropriately called "drab", and discreet Harris tweeds for the country. There was a little more choice in the summer, when white flannels and "boating jackets", fore-runners of the modern blazer, could be seen in the afternoons.

Such imagination as was allowed in men's fashion was confined to overcoats, which could be in a number of designs, and trimmed perhaps with fur or velvet on the collar, but which were still limited to the basic colours.

The travelling "Ulster", with caped shoulders, was popular. Sporting gentlemen might wear three-quarter length overcoats in very faintly striped smooth wool cloth, with velvet trimming on the collar. The "Raglan" coat was cut very full in the back, and was often made of water-proof material, though proper raincoats were as popular for men as they were for women.

A gentleman's underwear consisted of a vest and long pants in wool, silk or cashmere. A catalogue states, guardedly, of the cashmere underwear,

"unshrinkable so called". A cotton shirt with a high, starched collar was worn with a tie and jewelled tie pin. Gentlemen wore morning coats and trousers, woollen socks, highly polished shoes and spats. There was very little choice in hats. Top hats or bowlers were worn in town, and perhaps a tweed hat or cap in the country.

As internal combustion, the telephone and electricity arrived on the technical scene, new dance crazes arrived on the social scene: the tango, the Turkey Trot and the Bunny Hug. Serge Diaghilev influenced a whole school of design when his Ballets Russes arrived in Paris in 1909, and the brighter colours used by his designers, Bakst, Golovine and Benois, were en-thusiastically accepted for every-day wear. Women started to take an interest in more energetic sports. Tennis, swimming and even roller-skating began to be considered more ladylike than they had been.

Gradually, almost as if pre-paring themselves for the years of the Great War when they would have to work in factories, in offices and on public trans-

port, the women of the early years of the 1900s adapted their fashions to make them more suitable for busy working lives. They kept their silks, chiffons, taffetas and laces for the evening, when they went to theatres and receptions as bejewelled as ever.

Evening dresses, like day dresses, usually consisted of a bodice and skirt. Necklines were cut quite low and were filled in with tulle or lace. The skirts, with long trains, were often em-broidered with gold or silver beads. Very elaborate evening cloaks or capes were worn, made of velvet, silk, brocade or other expensive material, and trimmed with feathers, fur, lace and embroidery.

Boys were fitted out for school at one of the big stores spec-ializing in uniforms, and the level of the school could often be judged by the materials in which the uniforms were available. The "Eton" suit consisted of a short jacket, waistcoat and striped trousers. The jacket and waist-coat were made of vicuna. The trousers, however, were made of special "untearable" West of England cloth.

Motoring dress 1905 hat tied down with chiffon scarf

Knickerbocker suit for cycling. Straw hat, buttoned boots c. 1900

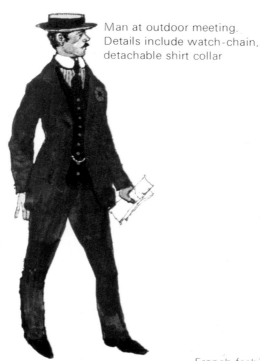
Man at outdoor meeting. Details include watch-chain, detachable shirt collar

French fashion 1914. White dress under caftan plus fur-trimmed coat

Colour

Clothes were usually of a subdued colour until about 1912. Black, black and white, navy blue, brown or dark grey were worn out of doors, and it was considered fashionable to use different shades of the same colour—starting, for instance, with pale green and shading through to a dark bottle green. Paler colours were worn in the evening, when the soft chiffons and laces were often in shell-pink, oyster or pale biscuit. These formal colours were forgotten in about 1912, when the influence of the Russian Ballet made itself felt, and brightly patterned silks were to be seen everywhere.

Cycling Suits

Bicycling was a very popular activity, and men could buy specially designed "cycling suits". A catalogue of 1913 enthuses about the virtues of wool for a cycling suit: "All perspiration is absorbed by hygienic methods and quickly evaporated, instead of being allowed to remain on the surface of the skin." The suit consisted of a Norfolk jacket and a pair of "knickers" in tweed or flannel, with a matching waistcoat and cap, and a pair of woollen stockings. Stiff collars and ties were worn, and waterproof ponchos could be bought for bad weather.

Gentlemen at Ease

At home, the Edwardian gentleman could choose from a large selection of smoking jackets, or dressing jackets or gowns. Smoking jackets had a slightly military look about them with their silk-cord frogging on serge or velvet. Dressing gowns could be in tweed, flannel, cashmere, serge, vicuna, camel hair or white towelling.

Motoring Outfits

For motoring, ladies wore huge linen dust coats over their dresses, tied their hats down with scarves or even wore exaggerated versions of men's capes, and hid their faces behind goggles. Protected in this way they felt ready to endure any hazard that the new-fangled motor car had to offer, as it sped along at fifteen miles an hour.

Knitted Garments

For sporting occasions women would often wear knitted sweaters, and belted cardigans like Norfolk jackets. These could be worn with tweed or plain skirts, slightly above the ankle, when out for a walk or a game of tennis or croquet.

Hats

At the beginning of the twentieth century small hats were in style, but as the hair styles changed so did the hats which went on them. Large "Merry Widow" hats became the fashion in 1907, when the designs inspired by Lehar's masterpiece gained popularity. These huge oval shapes were covered with "willow" plumes, and it was not unusual to see ostrich feathers or bird's wings, or large artificial flowers, making a fantastic, colourful pile on top of a carefully dressed head of hair. The hats were held on with long, viciously pointed hat pins, which found a fixing in the wads of false hair which padded out the natural hair. As it was considered improper for a woman to appear in public without a headcovering, these large hats became a nuisance in theatres, where they successfully obscured the view of people sitting behind them. First there were polite requests by theatre managers, and later strict laws were made to put a stop to the inconvience. As far back as 1895 the first night programme of Wilde's *The Importance of being Earnest* advertised among its seat prices "Upper Boxes, Numbered and Reserved (Bonnets allowed) 4s".

Motoring cap and goggles

Ladies' hats

Silver mesh purse

Caped overcoat

Smoking jacket

bowler hat

butterfly collar

silk cravat

morning coat

leather gloves

silver topped cane

striped trousers

spats

band box

parasol

ostrich feather hat

jacket

pleated front blouse

gathered skirt

walking suit

short train

walking boots

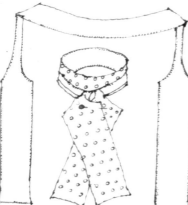

Cravat and method of tying

**Fashion is what one wears oneself.
What is unfashionable is what other people wear.**

Oscar Wilde: An Ideal Husband (1895)

Insect shaped filigree brooch

The Great War 1914–1918

Side-slit hobble skirt with short full tunic
France 1914

Fashion, as such, almost came to a standstill during the years of the Great War. Many young and middle-aged women worked in hospitals, factories and on public transport, and had no time to spend dressing themselves up during the day. The changes that had appeared in the earlier decade now became more obvious. Skirts were ankle length and no longer needed button boots to give an impression of modesty. Silk stockings were worn with day and evening shoes, and a lady's ankle might now be exposed to view without causing a scandal.

One very strange fashion which was introduced just before the war was the hobble skirt. It allowed a maximum width of seventy centimetres around the ankles. The skirt could be part of a dress, or might be separate and worn with a trim jacket and blouse. One of the more outlandish variations was the lampshade dress, worn in the afternoon for teas and dances. The hobble skirt was wrapped in such a way that it opened up in front to just below the knee. A top with an enormous, mid-thigh length skirt

was worn with it. The hem of the top skirt was stiffened to stand out all around.

Silk, in one form or another, was the most popular material for these dresses, and advanced manufacturing techniques had led to softer, more pliable fabrics. Raw or slubbed silks were made into summer suits. Crêpes, chiffons and soft satins were in demand for evening dresses. Lighter, more flowing dresses were introduced and women began to enjoy their release from the tight corsets of the previous century.

Corsets were still worn by many women, of course, but they were less ferociously boned. Suspenders had now become attached to the corsets, relieving women of one piece of clothing.

An active woman in 1916 might wear a walking suit of surprisingly modern design. It had a full skirt of black or navy serge; and a hip-length, matching jacket, with long, practical sleeves and a high collar. Long boots or shoes with leggings were necessary with this outfit. Although the ankle had achieved decency, showing the calf was not proper at all.

At home in the summer a hand-embroidered muslin or cotton dress could be worn. It had embroidered cuffs and sailor collar, and the skirt reached to about thirty centimetres above the ground.

More than anything, though, this was a time for uniforms. As the men left for the war their jobs as munitions workers, farmhands, ticket collectors and conductors on public transport were taken by women.

When women were admitted to the forces, at other than honorary levels, the officers were usually able to have their uniforms made in reasonably good material, but the other ranks had to put up with what they were given. The WRNS, Women's Royal Naval Service, wore ordinary clothes to begin with, and it was not until early in 1918 that uniforms of rough, heavy blue serge were issued. They consisted of long, button-through dresses with high necks and small versions of the male sailor's collar, heavy boots, black stockings and "pudding basin" black felt hats. Officers wore white shirts with black ties, tailored jackets, dark blue ankle

Uniform of Women's
Volunteer Motor Driver
Corps

Highland Scottish soldier
with kilt, sporran and
glengarry cap

English munition worker 1915

Netherlands 1914: officer's
(mounted artillery) shako

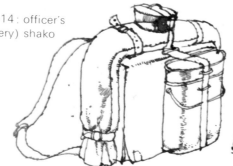

France 1914: soldier's
haversack and cap

Tunic of 2nd Lieut in
Hungarian infantry regiment
1914

French Cuirassier helmet,
canvas cover and horsehair
plume 1914

length skirts, and black velour tricorne hats with very wide brims: As if there was any likelihood of WRNS officers getting confused with their male counterparts, the badges of rank on their sleeves were in blue rather than gold.

A similar outfit in khaki was worn by the WAAC, The Women's Army Auxiliary Corps. The coat dress of the ranks was more tailored than that of the WRNS, and they had access to rather more comfortable fabrics.

Near the field of battle or in hospitals at home a familiar uniform was that of the voluntary Red Cross nurse. As the toll of wounded grew it became necessary to use volunteers to relieve the trained nurses, and many women joined the Voluntary Aid Detachment. The uniform consisted of a blue cotton dress, with a starched white cotton apron and headscarf, and stiff white collars and cuffs. A red cross was sewn on to the front of the apron.

Male uniforms were a good deal more splendid. Those of officers were covered in gold braid. The crack cavalry regiments still wore uniforms more

suitable for the days when war was an occupation for gentlemen. The tragic experiences suffered by these beautifully dressed and mounted men when they faced machinegun fire marked an end to the days of the cavalry charge. The tight breeches and boots, gorgeously frogged jackets, fur-trimmed pelisses and plumed shakos were given up for more practical outfits.

The ordinary British foot soldier wore a uniform of rough, khaki wool. It consisted of a jacket with a high, turn-over collar and four patch pockets, and trousers. These were bound from the knee down with puttees, bands of slightly elastic material that required great skill to put on. The most satisfactory way of getting wrinkle-free puttees was to damp them before binding them round the legs, but this could be uncomfortable if they shrank too much as they dried out. A peaked cap was worn with this uniform for parade or for marching, but steel helmets were worn in battle.

Officers wore uniforms cut on very similar lines, though of much better material, and they could usually afford to go to their

own tailors to be outfitted.' Over their jackets they wore Sam Browne belts of polished leather, with a pistol in a holster on the right hand side. The belt was named after its innovator, General Sir Samuel J Browne. An officer's boots were brown, as were his gloves, and, after a few attempts to go into modern battle with a sword, a wooden stick was carried as a badge of rank.

A much more colourful section of the British Army was the Scottish Highland regiments. They wore the traditional Highland garment, the kilt, made from woollen cloth, woven into the various patterns that are associated with individual clans. The regiments were named after the clans, and the soldiers wore the tartan of the regiment. Then, as now, officers wore scarlet jackets with plaids over the shoulders. Ordinary soldiers in battle wore khaki jackets similar to those of the English regiments. On active service, a khaki cloth apron was usually worn over the kilt, with a pocket in front to replace the traditional sporran, which is always worn with full dress.

US soldier with steel helmet, gas mask in front, trousers tied with puttees

Blue serge uniform of Women's Royal Naval Service 1918

Austria-Hungary; Hussar corporal in frogged "Attila", matching fur-trimmed pelisse

The German Air Force

Pilots in the German Air Force wore uniforms of field grey, trimmed with contrasting colours. One such uniform consisted of grey breeches and a jacket with a high, turn-over collar faced with dark green. There was red piping on the shoulder-tabs and round the edges of the peaked cap, which had a dark green band. Brown leather gaiters and boots were worn with this outfit. Another, rather more dashing, uniform had similar breeches worn with brown boots and grey puttees, and a jacket cut in the "lancer" style. It had a high collar and a shaped panel in the front, which buttoned on both sides. The collar, the front panel and the shoulder-tabs were all trimmed with yellow, as were the seams on the back of the jacket, and the peaked cap had a yellow band.

Hats

Women wore some very extraordinary hats just before the Great War. One of the most popular styles was a small toque, trimmed with enormous bird's feathers which towered forty-five centimetres or so above the head. Hats with a variety of brims were also trimmed in this way, and very often had small veils as well. With the advent of war, these hats were kept for smart occasions. For daily wear practical little plain felt hats were popular. Large veils were confined to the use of lady motorists, who feared that the dust and wind might damage their complexions.

Feather-trimmed toque hat Austria 1913

Policewomen

There are historical records of policewomen in England as far back as the reign of the first Elizabeth, though it is doubtful if the ladies in question wore a distinguishing uniform. The first women's police force was founded in 1914 by Miss Nina Boyle and Miss Margaret Damer Dawson, on a purely voluntary basis. The uniforms were a good deal better cut than those worn by the ranks of the armed forces, and were designed on the same lines as a WRNS officer's uniform. The senior officers wore peaked caps and other ranks wore hard felt hats with wide brims, designed to give protection from the weather and also from "a fairly sharp blow on the head."

America

The United States entered the war in 1917, and immediately began intensive efforts among the civilian population to raise money for the Red Cross and other organizations. Officers of the American Red Cross wore smart khaki raincoats over their skirts and jackets, and had match-ing forage caps. Polished brown leather boots and belts were also worn. Workers for the YMCA, which took mobile food wagons everywhere in the war area, wore practical dresses of wool or calico, and were, of course, never seen without hats.

Haute Couture

The great fashion houses in Paris such as Lanvin, Paquin, Worth, Callot Soeurs and Doeuillet did not stop designing and producing high fashion clothes during the war, though naturally their output decreased. Many rich and beautiful women still thought of Paris as the only place to get good clothes. One of Poiret's most celebrated customers was the famous spy, Mata Hari, some of whose dresses were designed by Romain de Tirtoff, better known as the artist, Erté.

Gas Masks

On April 22, 1915, at Ypres, poison gas was used for the first time as an offensive weapon. A mixture of chlorine and hydrogen peroxide was released into the atmosphere by the German Army, and caused considerable panic among the opposing forces. At first, the only sort of protection against the gas was a wad of cotton wool put over the mouth and held in position by a piece of muslin or old fashioned veiling. The soldiers also used to carry T-shaped sticks with little balls of cotton-wool hung from each arm of the T, to indicate the direction of the wind. If the wind was blowing away, the gas would be blown back to the enemy. Shortly after the first gas attack the M2 gasmask was issued. It consisted of a rubber mask with windows for the eyes, and a tube, which was attached to an air-intake container that held chemicals to neutralize those used in the gas.

German officer in "lancer front" jacket 1916

Policewoman—hard felt hat, laced boots

German gas mask

Straw hat, Vienna 1914

Hat of WVMDC (see previous spread)

British infantryman 1914

soft peaked cap, brass badge

khaki uniform, brass buttons, shoulder straps

ammunition pouches on webbing belt

canvas satchel for supplies

puttees wrapped around the leg

brown leather boots

Queen Alexandra's Imperial Military Nursing Service 1914-18

white cap derived from design by Florence Nightingale

uniform cape

large white apron with pocket

German other-ranks field cap 1914

For a short time policewomen were one of the sights of London, along with the Tower and Westminster Abbey.

Lilian Wyles (1918)

Austria-Hungary o/r field cap (cavalry) 1914

The Twenties

Golf wear; plus fours, brogue shoes, bow tie flat tweed cap

Any mention of the "Twenties" instantly conjures up visions of girls with very short skirts, no waists, shingled hair and long cigarette holders. These extremes of fashion did not take place immediately, however, for at the beginning of the decade Europe was still recovering from war. Although the shorter skirts, which women had got used to wearing during the war, were still worn, they were seldom more than twenty-two centimetres above the ground.

Young women, determined to keep their new-found freedom, banished corsets from their wardrobes. They wore petticoats of silk or *crêpe de chine* under their dresses, and paved the way for the flat-chested look, always associated with these years.

The garment that came into fashion for flattening the body and doing away with the waist was known as a corselet, a plain, silk tube held up by shoulder straps. It was succeeded by the camisole, which was a little more restricting; and then by a combination of camisole and knickers called "cami-knickers" or, for a short while, "cami-bockers". Silk

stockings were, once again, held up by suspenders attached to a separate belt, and "fast" women wore ornamental garters just under the skirt-line.

Rayon, or artificial silk, was introduced during the Twenties. Synthetic pearls were manufactured as well, which made it possible for girls to wear the fashionable long necklaces without spending huge sums of money. What is generally thought of as the "Twenties" look only lasted for a few years. In 1925 skirts were below the knee, and it was only in 1926 and 1927 that they were knee length. By 1928 evening dresses had started lengthening at the back.

One of the most famous creators of fashion at this time was Gabrielle, "Coco", Chanel. The simple skirts and pullovers, and classic suits, which she popularised, originally derived from outfits that she designed while working in a hospital at Deauville during the war.

The slim, boyish, fashionable figure required the shortest hair possible. Razor-cutting, a far more painful process than it is nowadays, was popular. Up to 1924 the hair was simply

bobbed, and then the shingle was introduced. For a short while the two styles were combined in the "bingle". If a girl's hair was naturally straight the waved look could be achieved at home with metal curling tongs, which were heated over little spirit stoves. If money was no object, one of the new "permanent waves" by Marcel or Vasco could be undergone at the hairdresser's. Marcel's version of the "perm" was so successful that artificially waved hair was referred to as "marcelled".

On top of the shingled hair went another trademark of the Twenties, the cloche hat. The style was introduced in late 1923, and did not go out of fashion until 1930. The cloche was the natural successor to the toque, which had lasted from 1913 right through the war and could still be seen, pulled further down over the forehead, in 1923. Gradually the toque became closer fitting and rounder on top. Then it acquired a small, turnback brim which came right down over the eyebrows. The cloche might be of felt or fine straw for daytime wear, and gold or silver lamé for the evening.

Evening suit with black trimming, white tie and stiff collar 1920

1921: lady in fur-trimmed coat-dress. She carries a pink raincoat

1921: two-colour dress with belt, vertical decorations. Fox fur wrap

Felt hat with large scarf

Cloche hat 1927

Hat with buckle 1926

It was often adorned with bunches of feathers at the side, which looked rather like small feather dusters. By the end of the decade the brim was turned down all round the hat, which began to look a little less like a helmet.

When styles of the Twenties were at their most extreme, as little as a metre of fabric was enough to make a skirt. Very often more was used and the skirt was carefully pleated. Striped wool jersey tops with matching scarves could be worn with these skirts. A pullover with a Fair Isle pattern was thought very smart with a skirt, and was worn for golf.

Evening dresses were made of silk, chiffon, georgette or muslin, and were often heavily embroidered with tiny coloured beads. A black net sheath, entirely covered with black bugle beads, could be worn over a black silk slip. Pale green georgette might be patterned with silver and white. The dresses were sleeveless, and usually had a little loop on the inside of the shoulder strap, to be fastened over the strap of the camisole to keep it in place.

A very popular variation for the evening was the dress with the "handkerchief" skirt. A dozen or so panels of chiffon or georgette were sewn around a band at the hipline of the dress, so that the points hung down below the hem. These dresses were often embroidered with beads around the neckline.

A certain amount of individuality was allowed in men's clothes at this time, although formal occasions called for formal wear. Dinner jackets were still thought unsuitable for anything but the theatre or suppers at home. Although the actor, Jack Buchanan, introduced the double-breasted dinner jacket in 1924, it was some time before it became generally popular. For receptions, the opera or ballet and for private dances suits of tails were considered essential. They were worn with starched white shirts and waistcoats, white bow ties and mother-of-pearl or jewelled links and studs. A white scarf might be worn, and a black, silk top hat. For visits to the opera or ballet a collapsible *gibus*, or opera hat, was more convenient. This was made in corded silk and was con-

structed in such a way that it could be flattened and, if necessary, sat on. It easily sprang back.

Except in places where morning clothes were still worn as a sort of uniform, such as banks or large shops, most men wore lounge suits for ordinary daytime occupations. Hats were universal. A young man without a hat was thought "erratic". Bowlers had taken over from top hats for general town wear, though a trilby looked better with a lounge suit, and cloth caps or boaters were worn for sport.

Probably the most extreme male fashion craze was that of "Oxford bags", trousers with immensely wide legs, cut so baggy that the turn-ups used to trail in the mud. They were noted at Oxford as early as 1922 when a young man, later to become a famous designer, wore a pair of Oxford bags with a scarlet pullover, a gold tie and fur gauntlets. It was not until the middle of the decade, however, that the fad really caught on with everyone else. The bags were usually made of pale grey flannel, or beige, which was a colour more or less invented in the Twenties.

Evening dress in sheer fabric with deep décolleté

Straw boater, blue blazer, white flannel Oxford bags, canvas shoes

France 1926—skirts now really short, showing rolled stocking tops

Evening outfit with "pearl" decoration, matching fur-trimmed cloak, 1926

Jewellery and Accessories

In addition to the long "flapper" necklaces that went with the short dresses, women wore bracelets—sometimes as many as six on the same arm. Cloche hats were ornamented with brooches, and handbags would contain cigarette cases, cigarette holders, and powder compacts. Compacts were sometimes made to be carried on their own: silver cylinders which unscrewed in the middle to reveal a tiny mirror, powder and a powder puff. At one end of the cylinder was a ribbon for hanging the compact from the arm, at the other a matching silk tassel which concealed a lipstick. Cigarette cases for both men and women might have Virginia cigarettes on one side and Turkish on the other. Pocket lighters were also carried. Wrist watches were still thought slightly "cissy" for men, and most men used a pocket watch, carried in the waistcoat.

France 1924/5
Egyptian-influenced jewelry
Gazette du Bon Ton

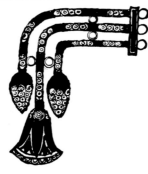

Tennis

One of the great heroines of the age was the French tennis player, Suzanne Lenglen. She played faster and more competitively than any woman had before her, and won six Wimbledon titles in six years. She usually wore a thin dress with a pleated skirt, white silk stockings rolled just below the knee—a fad which many girls copied—and white shoes. One of her customs was to wear an orange bandeau to keep her hair in place for the first match of the day, and change it for a crimson one for the second. The bandeau became so identified with her that cartoonists suggested that, if it slipped, tennis could change into blind man's buff.

Swimwear

Men's swimming costumes were uniformly dull at this time, cut in one piece out of navy blue or black wool. Only in the South of France was it thought proper to wear short trunks for swimming, and these could be in any colour. Women did rather better, being allowed striped wool costumes, or cotton shorts with a blouse top which came down to about hip level. Bandeaux were worn on the head or one of the new rubber bathing caps, but swimming was not a sport which was taken seriously, and few women cared to wet their hair. It was considered extremely smart to wear jewellery with bathing suits, and Kees van Dongen painted a swimsuited lady in 1924, blazing with jewels and obviously with no intention of going into the sea.

Striped belted swimsuit

Clinging bathing dress with daring lace fastening

Shoes

Men's shoes branched out a little from the very plain styles, familiar before the war, and young men took to wearing two-tone shoes. The light coloured upper was decorated with patterns in darker leather. Tan and white brogues known as "co-respondent" shoes were thought a bit fast, and suede was definitely effeminate. Shoes for women were made by great stylists such as Salvatore Ferragamo, and had "Louis" heels, and straps across the instep. Shoes were usually made of soft leather for daytime, though silk or brocade might be used for the evening. Both sexes wore stout leather brogues for golfing or walking.

Black-and-tan shoe 1924

Skin shoe 1924

Buckled patent leather shoe 1925

Cosmetics

Painting the face had been considered improper for many years, and was confined to actresses and ladies of easy virtue—often thought of as the same thing. The newly emancipated girls of the Twenties had no time for such nonsense. Two of the great beauticians, Helena Rubinstein and Elizabeth Arden, opened their salons and produced lotions and creams which sold in immense quantities. Both women started by using formulas from earlier times: Arden made a face cream supposed to be from a recipe of Madame Récamier; Rubinstein marketed a cream used by her mother, in Australia, to prevent sunburn. In addition to these, both firms produced lipsticks, powders and tonics for the skin. Oxblood was a favourite colour for lipstick, and very daring girls varnished their nails in the same colour.

The Movies

A young person's choice of clothes was often influenced by what the screen heroes and heroines wore. Stars such as Mary Pickford, Joan Crawford, Rudolph Valentino, Douglas Fairbanks and Jeannette MacDonald were as carefully and beautifully dressed off-screen as they were on. They could well afford it. Fairbanks, for example, was earning as much as £4,000 a week in 1926. The clothes for modern films were as up-to-date as possible, and introduced many new ideas, which were then passed on by tailors and dressmakers to their customers in other walks of life. Clothes for historical films were usually designed with some reference to current taste, resulting in some very peculiar costumes.

Fred Astaire in white tie and tails

long earrings

shingled hair

huge collar

white pearl motif

high collar, bare
bateau neckline
beneath

large red cloak

Loose jersey jacket,
black dress beneath,
quilted collar,
cuffs and hem

silk evening dress,
black and silver, with
long train

ankle length skirt

gold tassels on cloak

two-tone shoes with
large buckle and patent
toe

White hat with
cockade decoration 1922

**Give feminine fashions time enough and they
will starve all the moths to death.**

Detroit Free Press (1925)

Printed fabric for spring
dress to match the hat

The Thirties

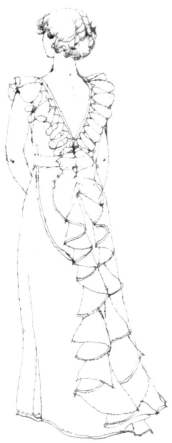

Pale blue evening dress with $\frac{1}{4}$-circle decoration France 1936

The New York Stock Market crashed in 1929 and the effects were felt throughout the world. The young people who had set the fast, jazzy pace of the Twenties were now grown up, and the juvenile high spirits which characterized the previous decade were replaced by a more adult outlook on life. Clothes became increasingly elegant, with the emphasis on quality and line rather than on shocking effect. Crazy dances like the Charleston and the Black Bottom gave way to the quickstep, and syncopated rhythms were less popular than the slower, more romantic tunes of Gershwin, Kern, Coward, Berlin and Porter.

The financial situation in America was so bad that the season after the market crash not one single commercial buyer went to Paris to look at the collections of the great fashion houses. This was the time when the most famous Parisian dress designers were doing some of their best work, and the houses of Chanel, Schiaparelli, Vionnet, Rochas, Patou and the American-born Mainbocher adapted their trading methods to the difficult times. Most of the big couturiers had made handsome profits during the Twenties, when money was plentiful, and they used their reserves to help themselves through the difficult years of the early Thirties. The clothes that they produced were all hand-made, so they did not have to worry about industrial problems. Most of the members of their staffs felt themselves part of a team and it was possible, therefore, to continue employing them on lower wages. All the little additions to a dress, the buttons, embroidery and trimming were done in small workshops which were privately run. The designers themselves agreed to considerable price cuts for their products, in order to keep trading. The textile industry formed a considerable part of France's economy and because of this, textile manufacturers were willing to give credit to the fashion houses. A successful design would promote the fabric as well as the dress.

In the circumstances it is a wonder that new styles appeared as soon as they did. The longer skirts, which began on evening dresses in 1928, became ac-cepted for everyday clothes a year later. In 1929 Madame Vionnet produced a day coat, reaching well down the calf, heavily trimmed with fox fur. In 1930 Marcel Rochas designed a tailored suit with a skirt five to seven centimetres below the knee, and a waist length jacket, which featured the very square shoulders that were to typify clothes of the late Thirties.

One of the most important designers of the time was Elsa Schiaparelli, who was born in Rome in 1896. Among her customers were the film stars, Garbo, Joan Crawford and Katherine Hepburn. They all wore the square-shouldered, long-skirted dresses in private life, and had other versions of them made for their films by Hollywood designers such as Adrian or Edith Head.

Obviously, only a small number of women could afford to have their clothes made at these exclusive houses. The Duchess of Windsor had her evening dresses made by Mainbocher. Famous beauties visited the collections each year to choose their new dresses. By the standards of today, the prices were am-

Race-going costume of 1930; large hat, long fur-trimmed dress

Informal outdoor tweed 1930. Waistcoat, breeches tucked into socks

Trousers appear for beach wear, with sun hat, France

Shirred evening cape
1933

Beret-type hat with
ribbon and scarf

Bathing costume

azingly reasonable. A plain dress by Vionnet cost as little as £19 in 1938, but a man could buy a tailored suit for about half that price.

There were alternatives for women who could not afford the trouble and expense of going to Paris to buy original creations. Magazines such as *Vogue, Harper's Bazaar, Vanity Fair* and *Femina* reproduced photographs of the latest styles, and most women with any taste knew a dressmaker "round the corner" who was expert at making up very presentable imitations of the latest fashion.

Trouser suits appeared at this time, made popular by the designer, Schiaparelli. What was acceptable in France, however, was not necessarily acceptable in England. When Schiaparelli went to London to buy tweeds for other clothes she was attacked in the Press. One English woman wrote to a paper, objecting that a "foreign woman should come here and dictate to us what we are going to wear," conveniently forgetting that what she was already wearing had probably been "dictated" by

Patou or Vionnet. The trouser suit was designed for all occasions: sport, travelling, evening wear and casual lounging pyjamas. Schiaparelli pointed out that in Middle Eastern countries women often wore trousers while the men wore robes, and that it was ridiculous to consider trousers immodest on women. A typical suit consisted of a blouse with a halter neck, wide trousers and a hip-length, belted jacket. A round, pancake hat might be worn with the outfit. Certain styles of millinery were the only part of fashion which did not seem to share the otherwise general elegance.

A variation on the trouser suit was seen in the striped cotton trousers and jackets which Mainbocher introduced— an early example of high fashion imitating workmen's clothes.

Masculine styles have always been slower to develop than feminine, and men's clothes changed very little during the Thirties. Some of the more extreme fashions were discarded, such as Oxford bags, though trousers remained wide. The

double-breasted lounge suit became more popular and was often worn without a waistcoat. The frock coat had gone out completely, and the trend towards more casual clothes continued. Morning coats were *de rigueur* for formal occasions. Black coats with striped trousers were worn for winter weddings. Matching grey trousers and coats were worn for weddings in the summer or for private enclosures at race meetings. Grey top hats were almost invariably worn with morning dress, with the exception of ambassadors on formal visits, who kept the black silk top hats.

"Sports" jackets with flannel trousers were becoming increasingly popular. The trousers were usually made of pale or mid-grey flannel, though occasionally fawn or sand coloured ones were seen. The jackets were of tweed, and might be in a variety of styles: with a half belt at the back and pleats in front, or quite plain, or collarless. Vents at the back were not usual in ordinary sports jackets. They were supposed to be confined to "hacking" jackets, worn with breeches or jodhpurs while out riding.

English schoolboy, 1939

Cloth-capped worker, collarless shirt, neck-cloth, England

England 1935—a Labour leader still wears formal dark clothes

1938—button-trimmed tabs, coatee with high shoulders

Foundations

The corset, so cheerfully thrown out by the young women of the Twenties, did not stay away for long, and the longer, sleeker lines of the dresses in the Thirties required a firm foundation. The one-piece corset was introduced in the early Thirties. It was made of light supple fabric which moulded the figure. Suspenders were attached to the corset. Towards the end of the decade there was an attempt to revive tight lacing, when frills and femininity took over from elegance for a short time before the outbreak of the Second World War.

1930 combined foundation garment

For golf; light jacket buttoned at waist, striped jersey underneath

Knitwear

Tweed, flannel or woollen skirts were very popular worn with jumpers, sweaters or cardigans. The jumpers often had short sleeves, and were belted with either a knitted band of the same wool or with a different fabric. Complete outfits might be knitted: skirts and jumpers or complete dresses, cardigans, matching handbags and berets.

Sportswear and Swimwear

The general emancipation of women led to a considerable relaxation in sportswear styles. As early as 1931 an American woman played tennis with bare legs rather than the obligatory thin white stockings, though it was not until 1933 that a girl dared to appear on the tennis court—again in America—wearing shorts above the knee. More women took to wearing breeches and boots for riding, though the riding habit was still considered essential on the hunting field. Backless bathing costumes of machine-knitted wool were popular. Alternatively, two-piece swimming costumes could be worn. Decorative rubber bathing caps were introduced in the Thirties. Cotton or linen beach slacks or wraparound skirts were worn with "beach jewellery" of painted wood or cork.

1930: white canvas beach hat with scarf

1932; small hat with veil, huge fur collar and fur on sleeves

Materials and Furs

Although natural fibres were still the most popular, there was a great increase in the use of artificial fabrics, rayon in particular. Some artificial fibres were mixed with natural ones to produce crease resistance. The zip fastener, set into the side or the back of a dress, often replaced the more old fashioned hooks and eyes, though zips were not yet used to fasten men's trousers. Furs were seen everywhere. Silver fox pelts, complete with heads, paws and tails, had a clip concealed in the creature's mouth which could be attached to a tab under the tail when the fur was worn around the shoulders. Huge lynx collars, as well as ocelot, leopard, pony skin, mink or musquash were all popular.

Ready Made Clothes and Toiles

The heads of the great fashion houses in Paris were not slow to realize that there was a large prospective market for ready-made copies of their designs. At one time, buyers from the large American stores had bought a dozen or so copies of the same dress direct from Paris, and then re-sold them, but customs duties were making this more and more expensive, and a new system was worked out. A single "toile", a design cut out of linen and supplied with instructions for making up, was bought by a store, and then simplified, copied and sold in thousands to enthusiastic customers. The various parts of the dress were marked out on thin paper in a patent ink which transferred to fabric when pressed with a hot iron, and the resulting shape could be cut out and made up at home.

Hats

Hats remained quite small in the Thirties, though they were no longer pulled down over the eyes. A simpler version of the cloche was still worn, however, made of felt with a narrow brim which might be turned down on one side. Other hats were much smaller, and came in a variety of shapes. Berets were popular with sports clothes, and the pill-box shape was made extremely fashionable by Princess Marina of Greece, who married the Duke of Kent in 1934. The Princess liked to wear large picture hats for formal occasions, a fashion which was also enthusiastically adopted. Women wore feminine versions of a man's felt trilby hat, sometimes decorated with a single feather, but more often left plain. The trilby was by far the most popular wear for men during the day, though men in the City kept their bowler hats, and black silk toppers were worn with evening dress. Black trilby hats might be worn with dinner jackets.

Gentlemen's tweed golfing cap

shirt with
stiff white collar

grey tail-coat with
matching trousers

small pillbox hat
with veil

Summer dress
in silk gauze with
black neck trim

loose sleeves with
floating points

sash

long black gloves

t grey top hat

fox fur with tail

black patent shoes

white shoes, black patent
heels and toes

Small hat with ostrich
plumes 1936

**An old suit, a battered hat, a perfect tie and
a good collar—that's what makes a well-dressed man.**

Baron de Meyer

Long white gloves 1932

The War Years 1939-1945

Pillbox hat, covered
with tulle and ribbons
France c. 1939

Uniformed nurse with
steel helmet

From the point of view of fashion, the years of the Second World War were marked by the necessity to economize. "Make do and mend" schemes were introduced and given wide publicity. Women were encouraged to adapt and remake old clothes, and dressmakers advertised their ability to "turn last season's dress into something new." Most countries had rationing schemes, based on a system of "points". So many points were allocated to each man, woman and child according to his or her needs. People who required special clothes for war work were able to apply for extra points, and other special cases had the same opportunity.

Clothes rationing was introduced in Britain in June, 1941, using a system which was already being applied in Germany. Each person was allowed a basic sixty-six points a year, from which to buy either made up garments or materials such as knitting wool. There was no real advantage in being able to make one's own clothes, as points spent on fabric were the same as points spent on ready-made clothes. The points were issued in sheets of paper coupons, from which the shopkeeper cut the required amount. A dress in fine wool might cost eleven coupons, while much the same thing in rayon cost only seven. Artificial fibres were more readily available than natural ones, though the factories were mostly turned over to war work. A woman's two-piece suit could cost anything between fourteen and eighteen coupons, while a man might give as many as twenty-six for a suit, and five for a pullover to go with it.

In 1942 a range of "Utility" goods was introduced in England. The idea was to economize even further on raw materials by producing clothing and household goods in standard patterns. A team of clothes designers was brought together and came up with a series of styles cut on very simple lines, with the minimum of trimming or decoration. These were then marketed at controlled prices, and everyone began to look as if they were in a kind of civilian uniform. Utility clothes, though serviceable and reasonably well designed, were cut from as little material as possible. Hems and seams were very skimpy, and pleats were carefully sewn to make them look fuller than they actually were.

Most men between the ages of eighteen and forty were in one of the armed forces. Those who were not did some other form of war work, either in the mines or on the land or in one of the Civil Defence organizations. Service uniforms had not changed a great deal since the previous war. The colours remained the same and the cut of the officers' uniforms stayed much as it was. Men in the ranks no longer had to bother with puttees, for trouser legs were now held in the webbing gaiters. The "blouson" style battledress was more appropriate to modern warfare.

When, and if, they got some leave men probably wore the clothes they had bought before the war started. If they had coupons to spare, however, they could buy themselves a Utility suit in grey, blue or brown woollen material. It was single-breasted, with a maximum of five pockets, no turn-ups and no metal fastenings—all metal was collected for the war effort.

Utility suit with
square shoulders,
short skirt

Slacks with duffle coat
and blouse

Khaki uniform of A.T.S.
small peaked cap

Light cotton field service cap, German Army

Ladies' gloves from Paris, late 1930s— 1940

Badge of Malta Command, British Army

German infantry uniform for a senior N.C.O.

Economy was the watchword and very few of these suits had waistcoats. Men wore sleeveless pullovers with V necks under their jackets. Even greater economy could be achieved by wearing a reversible pullover, perhaps grey or fawn on one side and lovat green on the other. Knitwear was usually in plain colours. Pale yellow was one of the most popular, closely followed by maroon and a very nasty, rusty brown colour.

Vests and underpants in wool or cellular cotton were worn, depending on the weather. Collar-attached shirts were now much more common, though starched white collars were still worn for more formal occasions. Belted or half-belted overcoats or raincoats were worn outdoors, and the felt trilby hat was almost universal. Material became increasingly scarce during the war, and a hat bought in 1939 probably had to last a good ten years. For men as well as women it was a case of having to have clothes and shoes repaired, cleaned or remade.

Such style as there was in women's clothes was achieved by very square, padded shoul-

ders on dresses and coats. Waists were belted and skirts came to just below the knee. Some of the fabrics, particularly the artificial ones, were richly, if not very tastefully, patterned. A bright green background, for instance, might be adorned with a pattern of flowers in pink and blue.

Hats took on a variety of strange shapes, and were the subjects of great ingenuity. In Paris during the German Occupation, for instance, women created hats from artificial flowers, some feathers, bits of veiling, lace and even wood shavings and scraps of newspaper. The idea, they said, was to throw the German troops off balance when they were confronted with these delightful confections. The Germans promptly countered this by forbidding the use of more than one bird per hat.

Felt hats were rather more down-to-earth, but no less remarkable in shape. There were wide-brimmed saucer shapes, and high, upturned flower pots with brims, often held on at the back of the head by a strap of the same material.

Knitting was a popular pas-

time, at home and during the hours spent in air raid shelters. Old garments were unravelled and the wool was reused. Multicoloured clothes were knitted from leftover scraps of pre-war wool. Complete dresses were knitted, or "twin sets" of shortsleeved jumpers and longsleeved cardigans.

Women's Utility suits were either of wool fabric or tweed, and had skirts forty-five centimetres from the ground. Jackets were usually hip-length, and might have either real or false pockets. Another version of the suit was the jacket dress. It was a complete dress with a high neck and a matching jacket, which could be worn outdoors with a fur stole. All designs were intended to be as multipurpose as possible. One Utility outfit of blouse, short jacket and skirt could be transformed into an evening dress simply by changing to a long skirt, and tying a sash round the waist.

Slacks were as popular as skirts for everyday wear, particularly among women who worked in factories.

US army battle dress

Dress of 1941, straw hat and veil, slingback heels

Officer of US Army Air Force

Statesman in black jacket, striped trousers, Homburg hat

Hair Styles

Men's hair was usually short and brushed flat on the head, held in place by brilliantine or one of a variety of hair creams. Some men wore moustaches, though the exaggerated "handlebar" moustache was generally confined to Air Force officers and a few Army officers fighting in the desert campaigns. Women wore their hair under turban scarves or held in net "snoods" during the day and while they were working. In the evening they either brushed it up on the top of their heads into a pile of curls, or swept it to the back into a roll, with another roll of hair on the forehead. The film star Veronica Lake wore her hair loose and shoulder length, parted on the left hand side and falling over the right eye, a style which became enormously popular.

Turban for day wear

Leisure time hair style

small high-crowned hat

Cinema and Theatre

Entertainment, in the theatre and the cinema, was very important for the morale of the troops and the civilians in the bombed cities of Europe. Hollywood stars such as Rita Hayworth, Susan Hayward, Veronica Lake, Greta Garbo and Merle Oberon wore the latest creations, and such advance in fashion as there was at the time was inspired by these glamorous women. Most of them did war work in their spare time, and had their uniforms made by top dressmakers — Gertrude Lawrence went to Molyneux for hers. Strapless evening dresses, which were not seen in England until the end of the Forties, were being worn in Hollywood films as early as 1942.

Home-made dress from improvised materials 1941

Shoes

Women's shoes cost five clothing coupons a pair, and, as leather was in short supply, were often made from tough fabrics and soled with rubber. For the evening or with smart clothes in the daytime a high heeled plain court shoe with a fairly high front was generally worn. For work flat-heeled, sensible shoes with crepe rubber soles and tie fronts were the most practical. Other variations were inspired by Hollywood. Raffia sandals with high cork platform soles and heels, or solid wedge soles, were derived from the preposterous styles worn by the film star Carmen Miranda.

Air Raids

Winston Churchill popularized the "siren suit", a one piece garment of woollen fabric with elasticated cuffs and ankles and big pockets. The feminine version also had a hood. It was extremely useful for wearing over nightwear or underwear when the air raid warning went. Many people chose not to undress fully at night, and went to the shelters in a variety of coats and wraps. Black or khaki fibre helmets could be bought to protect the head from falling debris, and the fashion-conscious could have these painted in the colour of their choice for a small extra charge. Gas masks in square cardboard boxes were issued, and children could have masks with "Mickey Mouse" faces. Fabric or imitation-leather covers were available for gas mask cases.

Child in gasmask 1941

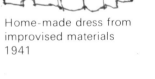

Casual platform shoes with back straps

Black evening shoe

Conversions

There seemed to be no limit to the number of garments which could be made into other garments, and the British Government invented a character called "Mrs Sew-and-Sew", whose advice was printed in newspapers and broadcast over the wireless. Old evening skirts, she said, could be made into slacks for wearing at home; 1930s top coats could be cut in half, and turned into outfits of skirt and bolero; and old curtains could be made up into "peasant" skirts. Patchwork became very popular, using up old scraps or offcuts of material, and, if all else failed, two coarse knitted dish cloths could be remade as a jumper.

Evening Wear

As most women had very little time at the end of the day to adorn themselves for parties, the most popular outfit for the evening was a blouse and skirt, long if for a dinner party, short if for a cocktail party. Many of the long dresses bought before the war lasted until the end of it, with a little help from the dressmaker. Trimming was sewn on or taken off to change the style. Moss crêpe, which hung in soft folds, was a fashionable material, though it was still possible to buy some silks and satins. The colour scheme of a wartime dinner dress might be emerald green or vivid magenta, decorated with gold sequins and paillettes.

Evening dress c 1941 black wool decorated with white beads

France 1940

flower-pot hat matches jacket

square-shouldered jacket, two patch pockets

tight sleeves

buff leather shoulder bag

knee-length skirt

court shoes

blue-grey cap with gilt metal badge

blue-grey uniform with patch pockets

R.A.F. officer England 1941

non-uniform spotted scarf

leather flying jacket sheepskin lined

uniform trousers tucked into boots

fur-lined zip-up flying boots

Shoulder badge "Desert Rats" (7th Armoured Division, England)

cer's summer cap, man Air Force 1942

In time of war, uniforms and working clothes are the height of fashion.

P. Gaule

The Post-War Era 1945–1960

Just as the First World War finally brought about the end of a leisured society, so World War II changed the social structures of most of the countries of the civilized world. The invention of the atom bomb, and other innumerable scientific and technical discoveries, gave a sense of urgency to the post-war years. Jet travel and advanced methods of communication demanded clothes that were functional and convenient. If they could be decorative at the same time so much the better, but comfort and usefullness came first.

This, however, did not happen at once. The first reaction of fashion designers at the end of the war was to recreate as much luxury as possible with the very limited resources that were available to them. Within a few months of the liberation of Paris a young designer named Christian Dior, who had worked with Pierre Balmain for the house of Lucien Lelong, started to design dresses with longer skirts. In the spring of 1947 he announced the creation of his "New Look", which caught on instantly and became universal fashion. The main characteristics of the New Look were the tight waist and

the much longer skirt, reaching to twenty four centimetres from the ground. All the padding was taken out of the shoulders, and the top half of the body, at least, presented a much more natural line. The first New Look skirts were very full, and required a number of petticoats to hold them out. They also needed a great deal more material than the British Government thought proper. Appeals were made to women not to wear the new fashion, but after years of austerity the temptation was too much. A Dior evening dress, photographed for *Vogue* in 1947, had over sixty metres of pleated chiffon in the skirt.

The New Look did not last long, however, and other designers soon brought out ideas of their own. As well as Dior, the top names in Paris were Fath, Balmain, Grès, Lanvin-Castillo and Balenciaga, who produced a rival to the New Look with his "sack" or "chemise" dress. This was considered very startling when it first appeared in 1951. It was a throwback to the Twenties with a loose top and a belt round the hips, though the skirt was calf length. The main problem with the sack, as with

the New Look, was that it looked wonderful on tall, slim girls with the beautiful figures of fashion models, but less than wonderful on the average housewife.

High fashion began a trend at this time that has continued ever since: creating a few model dresses for a few very rich women and allowing them to be used as inspiration for other designers. In this way, cheaper styles are produced that follow the main dictates of fashion, and which contrive at the same time to be wearable by ordinary people.

Life magazine proudly announced that manufacturers in New York started "cranking out" copies of Dior dresses three months after the New Look appeared in Paris, and could produce up to a million dresses a week with their high speed methods. By using cheaper materials, such as rayon instead of silk, and cutting down the metreage, a copy of a $450 Paris original could sell in Paris, Arkansas, for as little as $14.95.

Men leaving the armed forces had to make do with clothes issued by the Government on demobilization. These were notorious for their lack of style. Clothes rationing in England

Double-breasted overcoat wide-brimmed grey felt hat c. 1955

"New Look" evening dress c. 1950, strapless long gloves

"Trapeze" dress of 1958

The sack dress France 1958

Hat from France
c. 1958

Long gloves were popular

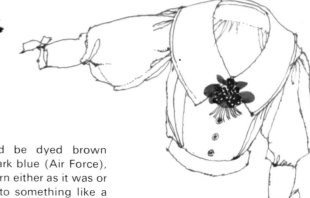
Puffed sleeves and wide-collared décolletage of the early 1950s

lasted until 1951, so there was not much opportunity to improve on the "demob" issue.

In the 1950s, however, a strong move back to elegance was started. Successful actors and men-about-town gave the lead with narrow trousers, coloured waistcoats and high lapels on their jackets. Any pattern could do for a waistcoat. Stiff white collars gave the outfit an Edwardian look that was increased by ties, which, according to a magazine, placed "the accent on silver and grey checks." Plain shirts were more usual, reportedly because patterned ones were expensive.

Evening dress remained "conservative, because," according to a contemporary source, "it is the function of men's evening clothes to enhance their partners' dresses." Some variations were noted. One man wore a plum coloured waistcoat with matching jacket cuffs, but "he looked like one of the band boys."

Lower down the social scale, however, strict rules did not apply, and there was a very popular fashion for "Teddy Boy" suits. Every Saturday night the dance halls would be crowded with young men dancing to the sound of music made popular by Johnny Ray, Nellie Lutcher and the Everly Brothers. They wore jackets that were a cross between Edwardian elegance and the American drape. Colour was important. Blue, maroon, yellow or red jackets had black velvet collars and cuffs. Trousers were of the stove-pipe variety, and shoes, which could also be very colourful, had thick soles of crepe rubber. Shirts with long, pointed collars were worn with black string or ribbon ties. Hair, which was grown fairly long, was greased and then brushed back into wings on either side, ending in a point on the nape of the neck, the "D A" style.

Less fashion-conscious men took advantage of the large number of army surplus stores that opened up at the end of the war, and the naval "duffle" coat became very nearly a uniform for students. It was not considered correct to wear the uniforms of the armed forces unless one was actually serving, but many dyed or altered garments owed their origin to the Army or the Air Force. The favourite for the treatment was the greatcoat, which could be dyed brown (Army) or dark blue (Air Force), and then worn either as it was or cut down into something like a naval reefer jacket.

The influence of the American presence in Europe and increased travel had a marked effect on clothes for the young. Blue jeans, which had been worn by American farm workers for generations, and which had become accepted casual wear for children and teenagers in the States, were first seen in England in about 1946. They looked somehow exotic and workmanlike at the same time. A year later, however, they were given the seal of approval when the Duke of Edinburgh wore a pair of blue jeans at a square dance that he and Queen Elizabeth II attended on their honeymoon. The original version of what has now become a fashion garment was held together at strategic points with copper rivets. The important thing was to buy the jeans a size too large and then shrink them to the body so that they fitted perfectly.

Multi-coloured wide ties were sometimes worn with Ted outfits 1958

1956: pony-tail hairdo full skirt covers stiff petticoats

Western-influenced casual wear, checked shirt, jeans c. 1956

Teddy boy: string tie, fitted jacket with velvet trim, drainpipe trousers

Fabrics

Nylon had already been used for making parachutes and, at the end of the war, triangular panels of this material were sold, coupon-free, and proved very popular for blouses, underwear and childrens' clothes. Other synthetic fabrics, such as terylene, were introduced in the early fifties, their main claim being that they allowed the body to breathe, which nylon did not. A drawback of all the man-made fibres was that after a time they became dull-looking and a man's white shirt took on a depressing pale grey look. Popular natural fabrics included tweed, for men's and women's coats and suits; silk, taffeta, chiffon and organdy for evening dresses; and cotton for shirts and blouses. Softer colours came back after the war, and black and white was considered one of the smartest mixtures for women's clothes.

Hats

From 1945 onwards it became more usual to see both men and women without hats in public, though many women thought it wrong to go hatless during the day. Hats, for the most part, were fairly small. A red straw creation by Dior was described in a magazine as "just like a little roof for the head." The usual shape was round and flat, perched straight on the top of the head. Larger, brimmed hats were tipped back a little. For dressier occasions, little straw pill-boxes covered with flowers were worn, or wide brimmed hats of transparent straw, decorated with feathers or flowers. Men wore hats much less frequently, though the trilby and the bowler were still popular, and the black felt homburg was worn with semi-formal clothes.

Beach Wear

Then, as now, America was the place where many of the new fashions in beach-wear started, and the magazines were full of hints on the right things to wear in Palm Beach or Malibu. Swimming costumes were often strapless, with a boned bodice to help them stay up. Materials such as denim, towelling or cotton piqué might be used. An outfit of shorts and a loose, zippered jacket could be made from bright green sackcloth. A mixture of flannel and wool jersey, in bright pink, could be made into "Bermuda" shorts and matching top. The Twenties' fashion of wearing jewellery with bathing costumes was carried a step further, and coral or turquoise beads were sewn directly on to the fabric.

One-piece swimsuit, towelling beach coat USA

Evening Dresses

If the function of men's evening clothes was to "enhance their partners' dresses," the partners took full advantage of the situation, and evening dresses in the early fifties were among the most romantic ever seen. Bodices were tight and usually sleeveless, though some gowns had elbow-length sleeves, and were often heavily embroidered with crystal beads. Huge skirts of tulle, slipper satin or taffeta were held out by large petticoats. Beadwork and embroidery came back into fashion to an extent not known for thirty years. The men were still expected to wear tail suits for very formal occasions, though double-breasted dinner jackets, without waistcoats and with soft fronted shirts, were seen more and more often.

Jewellery and Accessories

The low, strapless necklines of women's evening dresses required no more than one or two strands of real or imitation pearls worn as a choker, and very often even this was considered unnecessary. There was a fashion for wearing three strand bracelets on one wrist, on top of long gloves, if gloves were worn. Earrings or clips were generally small, though there were some American-inspired flower earclips worn with summer dresses. The "New Edwardian" men wore watchchains over their waistcoats, often with gold seals hanging from them; carried cigarette holders and very tightly rolled umbrellas, some of which were not unrolled even in a downpour; wore handstitched leather gloves; and sported carnations or roses in their buttonholes.

Winter Sports

Skiing and bobsledding, which had been popular before the war, began to come back into fashion in the Fifties. A recommended outfit for a skier "at more than 1,500 metres" was a pair of black and white houndstooth check trousers tucked into heavy black ski-boots, a woollen shirt with a stand-up collar and a yellow nylon or cotton poplin "blouson" jacket. Black gloves and a dark green wool cap with a long tail which, wrapped round the neck as a scarf, completed the ensemble. Tartan ski-trousers were thought a good idea as one could wear them, without gaiters, for "après-ski". If a full change for the evening was necessary, however, a mock-Austrian outfit, of brown knee breeches, grey shirt with a black ribbon tie, red waistcoat, short grey jacket lined with the same colour as the waistcoat, and white knitted wool socks, was considered the very last word.

Ski outfit c. 1956

Wide-brimmed hat deep décolletage early 1950s

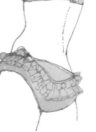

1959 bikini with frills

Cloche hat c. 1950

High turban hat France 1958

large-brimmed hat
pushed back on head

"Electric" blue jacket
velvet collar and cuffs

shirt with long pointed
collar, frills, string
tie

stand-up collar

black gloves

Dress by Dior

double-breasted fancy
waistcoat

narrow waist

shirt is straight but
has flying panels at
back

tight trousers

large turn-ups

crepe-soled shoes in
two-coloured suede

light grey shoes

**The only women who dress to please their husbands
are wearing last year's clothes.**

Anon

Cross-strapped shoe
France 1950

Toque hat
France 1950

The Sixties and After

Beatle-inspired fad for old military jackets

There have been an overwhelming number of changes in fashion since 1960. The mini-skirt, the maxi-skirt, the see-through blouse, hot pants, the "granny" look, the "beatnik" look and many others have all been seen in the past fifteen years. Probably the main reason for the different styles is that the people who dictate the fashions are no longer the same. The real power of the Paris *haute couture* houses ended when their designers realized that women were no longer content to be used as clothes hangers, and that most of the money in modern times belonged to a fast-moving set of young people who had very firm ideas of their own about what they wanted to wear.

Some of the younger designers, such as Yves St Laurent, Ungaro, Paco Rabanne and Courrèges, started designing clothes with an eye to an imaginary future, using linked metal discs and chain-mail for dresses, and silver or gold leather for boots and blouses. Rabanne is credited with the invention of the mini-skirt, which to begin with was short only in comparison with earlier styles, but which later rose to surprising heights.

Designers began to market sidelines. Dior sold perfume and sunglasses, Fath made ties, St Laurent designed towels, and many of the top couturiers opened up new markets with designs for men's clothes.

The centre of fashion, however, was London. The almost legendary popularity of the Beatles and other groups had led to a glorification of youth which the young English designers used to inspire a completely new idea of what to wear. The leader of this change was Mary Quant. She opened a small shop in King's Road, London, in 1955 and in 1963 got together a team of designers known as the Ginger Group. They produced simple, colourful, casual clothes for girls in their teens and twenties, with matching stockings and underwear, and even makeup. Skirts were short, sometimes very short, and stockings were replaced by tights. Underwear was reduced to the minimum.

While Mary Quant introduced an altered appearance for girls, John Stephen did the same for young men. Trousers, which had been tight in the fifties, now blossomed out with bell-bottoms. Shirts were cut from as little material as possible in the body and sleeves, though collars were usually quite large. The masculine outline seemed to undergo a change. A new shape appeared, which would have looked as odd in the tweeds and flannels of the thirties as a youth in 1935 would have looked in the slim-hipped, skimpy clothes of the late sixties.

In 1966 a style was introduced by Newman, in Paris, which combined two ideals. It allowed girls to wear practical, unfussy clothes and at the same time it suited the slim, youthful lines of the modern young man. It was "unisex", a whole range of clothes which could be worn equally well by either men or women. The only condition was that both sexes should be young and slim. Unfortunately that did not prevent a number of middle-aged couples, who should have known better, from trying to squeeze into clothes which only made them look ridiculous. The cult of youth spread to the people who worked in the businesses which supported it:

Mini-dress, France 1966 high soft leather boots

Hot pants with cap and long white plastic boots England 1971

"Gipsy" look for Pop festival. Loose blouse, beads, Indian skirt

Pop fan with face and glasses decorated with paint

Felt hat and sunglasses

Motorcyclist in self-decorated jacket with chains, buckles, studs

record producers, advertising executives, pop impresarios and trendy clothes-designers.

The human figure, unless very carefully looked after, begins to take on an unattractive shape after the middle thirties, and the desire for people to stay thin caused a rash of fashionable diets, sauna baths and keep-fit clubs. Although, in the seventies, women are supposed to be liberated, there is still a flourishing market in foundation garments, and advertisements for supports to make a man's figure look more youthful can be found every day in the newspapers.

Unisex designs included shirts, trousers, shoes, jackets, ties and cravats. Although the main garments might be made from a choice of materials, the one most frequently used was blue denim, which began to be popular at the end of the war. Jeans, shirts, blouson or long jackets, complete unisex suits, boleros, skirts, waistcoats and shoes have all been made from denim, either plain or with contrasting stitching around the edges. Brand new denim garments were originally not considered chic. At the beginning of

the craze the wearers went to great pains to fade and shrink their jeans, but soon denim clothes were available ready-faded and even frayed in appropriate places.

Designers in the sixties and seventies seemed to think it necessary to produce new ideas every year, in order to keep up with a seemingly endless demand for ready-made clothes. Some of the designs were not very practical. Some have seemed downright unattractive. The mini-skirt, which was really only successful if a girl had very good legs, was followed by the maxi-skirt. As this was usually made of fairly thick material, it was warm in winter, but got damp round the edges in rain or snow. Although it was a godsend to girls with less than perfect legs, it was not the ideal garment to wear when running through a crowded street for a bus. In between the mini and the maxi came the short-lived midi-skirt.

There has been a movement in the past twenty years to question, and often to do away with, many of the rules and standards that formed the basis of old-

fashioned society. The rules that used to apply to clothes and the use of material and colours are no longer thought relevant. In the Thirties and Forties the maxim "red and green, not fit to be seen" was taken seriously. A smart man would never have worn a spotted tie with a check or striped suit. In the Seventies any combination of colours or patterns is acceptable.

Now that the "swinging" Sixties are over there is, in fashion as well as in entertainment, a feeling of nostalgia, a looking back to the recent past when things were supposed to have been so much better. It may be that the designers of women's clothes have at last run out of original ideas, and are afraid of being thought conventional. Women have been encouraged to wear "Thirties" styles, though unfortunately modern imitations do not achieve the wonderful sleek look of that time. The Thirties designs, so beautifully designed and cut, were a logical progression from the Twenties. Their transition from fashion magazines to current use is seldom successful.

Pop star wearing fancy zip-up boots

Costume by Renée of London 1969

Pop musician in hippy clothes with beads

Yves St Laurent's blazer with pleated skirt 1971

Materials

Although a number of very successful man-made fabrics have been on the market for some time, wool, cotton and silk have kept their popularity. Synthetic materials are now much softer, and can be made up to look very like natural ones. They can have their disadvantages, as one film designer discovered when he tried to buy materials in America for making convicts' outfits. It was found impossible to "break down" the synthetic material in order to make it look worn and dirty, and finally the actor/convicts were dressed in material specially imported from France. The increasing awareness of the decline in the world wild animal population has led to a very large business in fake furs, some of which are intended to look as much like the real thing as possible; others, in bright, unnatural colours, are presented for exactly what they are.

Ethnic Clothes

Faster and easier world travel, and the popularity of the package holiday, have led to the introduction of many foreign styles into European wardrobes. Probably the most frequently seen is the caftan, worn by both men and women, derived from a North African garment. European men usually wear the caftan at home, but many women wear beautifully embroidered silk caftans for dinner parties or visits to the theatre. Cheese-cloth shirts, sometimes embroidered with coloured silks, have been brought back from India and Afghanistan, and some western women rather unadvisedly wear colourful Indian saris.

Hair

For the first time in almost two hundred years, men allowed their hair to grow long, though shorter hair is also acceptable. Like most fashions, long hair produced its reaction. Some young toughs went to the opposite extreme, and had their hair cut very close to their heads, earning them the name "skinheads". Most girls preferred their hair long and straight in the Sixties, though each new year a new "fashion" look would be created by one of the top coiffeurs.

Evening Clothes

Great individuality is still allowed in evening wear. Young women who can afford to do so wear beautifully finished, hand-made dresses by such designers as Zandra Rhodes, Bill Blass or Bill Gibb, and their escorts may wear tailored velvet or satin suits. The conventional dinner jacket is still popular, though it often appears in colours other than black. Velvet smoking jackets with black trousers are no longer confined to parties at home. No matter how practical clothes become for daytime wear, it seems that people will always want to dress up for the evening.

Sportswear and Beachwear

As sport becomes more and more competitive, speed becomes essential, and sports clothes are designed to fit as close to the body as possible. Football is played nowadays in shorts which would have been thought indecently brief forty years ago, and tennis and squash clothes combine comfort with minimum of material. Cotton is the best material for sports shirts, as it absorbs perspiration better than a synthetic fabric, but most shorts are now of man-made materials, and are consequently much easier to keep clean. Beachwear as well has been reduced to the minimum, the "bikini" being worn by both sexes.

Shoes

As many shoe fashions as dress fashions have been thought up in the Sixties and Seventies, though few of them are as elegant as the plain court shoe. Boots were essential with the mini-skirt, and Courrèges designed white boots with square toes and low heels to go with the outfits which he produced. There was a fashion for shoes with high, square, chunky heels. One fashion fad—without the excuse of keeping skirts out of the mud—was for platform soles, sometimes two or three inches thick.

Middle Eastern embroidered cotton dress, early 1970s

Girl with mock Red Indian hairstyle, bead headband 1974

The "unkempt" look—long-haired boy

Blue velvet jacket, worn with frilled shirt, bow tie 1976

Black and white leather boot by Ascher c. 1962

"Le minimum"—what is left of the bikini by 1976

Custom made platform shoe, leather, 1975

Girl, England 1976

short fringed
hair style

amber earrings

brown silk quilted
waistcoat, edged with
passementerie

pleated wool dress,
Liberty print

high-heeled soft
leather boots

Dark blue decorated
sunglasses

Boy's outfit, Italian
1973

printed cotton shirt

broad silk tie
by Valentino

handkerchief
matches colours
of tie

beige wool
sports jacket

light flannel
trousers

light tan leather
shoes, crepe soles

**Nowadays you can't tell whether a girl is wearing
a high mini-skirt or a low lobster-bib.**

Anon

Wooden bead necklaces

137